Designing and Planting Borders

Designing and Planting Borders

ROGER HARVEY

THE CROWOOD PRESS

First published in 2011 by
The Crowood Press Ltd
Ramsbury, Marlborough
Wiltshire SN8 2HR

www.crowood.com

© Roger Harvey 2011

British Library Cataloguing-in-Publication Data
A catalogue record for this book is available from the British Library.

ISBN 978 1 84797 311 5

Picture credits
Cotswold Garden Flowers, Old Barn, Station Road, Fladbury, Pershore, Worcestershire WR11 7EZ; Harpur Garden Images, Cannels Ash Farm West, Pentlow CO10 7JT; Harveys Garden Plants, Great Green, Thurston, Bury St Edmunds, Suffolk IP31 3SJ

Typeset by Jean Cussons Typesetting, Diss, Norfolk
Printed and bound in India by Replika Press Pvt Ltd

CONTENTS

DEDICATION

This book is dedicated firstly to Teresa, my wife; it would not have been possible to write this text without her enduring support and faith whilst we run our nursery Harveys Garden Plants. Secondly to my children, George, Rose and Milly who have been a great help over the years. I would also like to acknowledge my good friend Marcus Harpur, who unwaveringly provided many of the amazing photographs, and remember the late Richard Stubbs who encouraged me to redesign his own garden and then start my nursery business.

FOREWORD

Having for several years admired the author's nursery exhibits at the Royal Horticultural Society's flower shows, especially at their premier show Chelsea, I have come to recognize and respect two things. First, his enthusiasm for growing plants, perennials especially, in an ever-expanding variety. Secondly, his eye for colour and shape and his talent for bringing them together in a given space to create a look and a sense of harmony.

Though not without an element of surprise, Roger's borders, large and small, are full of promise and at the same time a feeling of confidence. This comes from his long experience of growing plants and from his abilities as a propagator, which involves handling plants, root, shoot and seed, and raising them from scratch. Added to this is his passion for sharing plants and with them the pleasures and satisfaction that all true hands-on gardeners enjoy.

It was in April 2011 that I paid my first visit to his nursery in Suffolk, having threatened it for some time. I wasn't sure what I would find, though I knew what to expect. Happily, I found what I expected and thus spent a most enjoyable day among the flowers and foliage of a stunning range of plants, some familiar, others quite new to me. Many of the plants I admired that day are included in the descriptions, photographs and most helpfully in the planting plans included here. They illustrate in a simple, effective and reassuringly practical way how first time or even long time gardeners might establish a new border or else revitalize an old one.

The practicalities of soil and aspect are of prime importance if one's dreams are to be fulfilled and this is where Roger's experience comes to the fore, providing the reader with suggestions, examples and advice to help make dreams become reality. Being a plantsman by nature and a designer only where space allows, I was particularly interested in Roger's choice of plants. Tough, easy, reliable plants can sometimes be boring but a careful look at those recommended in this book reveal a refreshing mix of proven favourites many of which are holders of the RHS Award of Garden Merit (AGM) and a healthy selection of newer arrivals which are now making their mark on today's garden scene.

One thing is certain, that there are now more plants available to gardeners than at any time previous, which I believe is good news despite what some pundits might say. The key to choosing the right plants for the right place, for first time gardeners certainly, is having the right advice and guidance to call upon which is why this most helpful and opportune book deserves to be read and its recommendations enjoyed.

Roy Lancaster
2011

INTRODUCTION

You can get an enormous amount of enjoyment and satisfaction from a well-designed border, especially if you are its creator.

Whether you have a whole new garden for which to provide plants, or your old border is looking tired and dated, or you just have some new ideas you want to introduce, this book provides a wide range of planting examples, with comprehensive detailed advice in the later chapters on how to select plants for a variety of aspects and soil types. The main focus here is given to soft landscaping – choosing the plants to suit your site conditions and placing them where they will please you most.

With gardens becoming increasingly smaller, and gardeners having less time to maintain them, one of the key factors in a modern garden is the creation of an interesting and pleasurable space without the worry of constant upkeep. With this in mind I have provided planting schemes for borders that are full of both shrubs and perennials – giving year-round colour without the need to replant with annuals.

In this age of sustainable ecosystems, birds and insects all need food to sustain them, and your planting should reflect this if possible. For example our native guelder rose, Viburnum opulus, a common constituent of mixed hedges in the countryside, has wonderful white heads of flowers in May followed by clusters of rich red berries in autumn. Many of our native birds and migrants such as blackbirds, mistle thrushes, redwings and fieldfares delight in this ample food-source in autumn and early winter.

Sitting in a quiet part of the garden and enjoying the plants and life brought into the environment by clever planting is spiritually uplifting, especially for a gardener. Whether your garden is small or extensive, the same principles apply to help you get the most from your garden and achieve maximum enjoyment from this space during precious times of relaxation.

LEFT: *Viburnum opulus* spring flowers. (Harpur Garden Images)
MIDDLE: *Viburnum opulus* autumn berries. (Harpur Garden Images)
RIGHT: *Viburnum opulus* autumn leaf colour. (Harpur Garden Images)

OPPOSITE: High summer – a riot of colour. (Harveys Garden Plants)

1 REVAMP OR NEW BORDER?

The first question to ask is what exactly are you hoping to achieve in your garden? Is the plan to revamp existing borders or to start from scratch with a new garden? Once this has been decided, you can move forward.

REVAMPING EXISTING BORDERS

Revamping existing borders may be a worthwhile and necessary exercise, especially when over-enthusiastic gardeners have planted shrubs and perennials incorrectly. There are a number of reasons for deciding on a revamp.

Plant Size

The original gardener may not have taken into account the eventual plant size, with the result that they are now too large. You may have several shrubs or perennials planted too closely together, with a tendency to form a hedge rather than maturing to specimens of individual beauty. Someone may have fallen in love with a particular shrub and decided to plant it regardless of its eventual size, probably thinking that it would be pruned regularly to contain its growth.

Wrong Position

Sometimes plants are planted in the wrong position, that is, shady perennials planted in sun or vice versa. This can often result in poor flowering. If a sun loving plant is planted in shade then the plant will make a bold move, by growing towards the sun. The resultant growth is weak and spindly as the branches arch to reach more light.

Overgrown Trees or Shrubs

Trees planted in small gardens have to be chosen carefully, both for size and position. Generally

An overgrown border.
(Harveys Garden Plants)

OPPOSITE: Grasses, especially *Miscanthus cultivars* look stunning planted close to buildings.

they should be planted not less than 5m from a new house, and rather more if the house is a few centuries old with poor or very little foundations. For example it is often tempting to plant fig trees (*Ficus carica*) in a warm spot supported by a neighbouring wall. These trees can grow up to 3m per year and can reach a colossal size.

Although fig trees respond well to pruning, the root system is extensive and can cause subsidence. Tree roots may also penetrate drains and cause blockages. Shallow rooting trees such as *Betula* species (birch), *Sorbus* species (rowan) and *Fagus* species (common beech) are especially troublesome. These trees will also cause uplifting of tarmac drives, pathways and slabs.

Large trees planted close to the house also give considerable shading. This may not be desirable especially if the property is old and with small windows.

Another point to consider is the proximity of your trees to a neighbour's house. The same planting rules apply, and if your tree causes damage to a neighbour's property then you will probably be liable for subsidence and any other damage caused. Will your household insurance cover it?

So, large trees with extensive root systems should be removed, if planted close to the house. Of course the same should apply to large shrubs that are left to become more or less trees. A good example of such is the *Corylus maxima purpurea* (purple leaved hazel). This will grow up to 5m+ in height and is often referred to as a small tree. If this shrub is coppiced (the stems cut back to the base), which is often carried out to maximize the purple colour of the leaves on the young growth, it will produce new stems up to 2m each year.

Before removing the offending tree or trees it is advisable to consult a qualified tree surgeon to give their expert opinion, and also obtain the necessary approval from the local planning authority in case the tree has a tree preservation order (TPO) which restricts pruning and felling. Even if your tree does not have such an order placed on it, you may live in a conservation area, which again restricts the work that can be carried out on the tree. If you decide to fell the tree, wherever possible plant another tree to make up

for the loss, and ensure that is of the appropriate size for the garden.

TREE PLANTING DISTANCE FROM HOUSE

A good rule of thumb to apply with regard to the planting distance from a house or brick wall is as follows. You should determine the mature size of the desired tree (*Betula utilis* 'Jacquemontii', for example, grows to 20m) and then plant no closer than its mature height. So if you were to consider planting a *Betula utilis* 'Jacquemontii', this fine tree should be planted about 20m from your house, other building or brick wall.

Time for a Change!

Sometimes you decide to revamp a border just for a change. Maybe new plants have been introduced that offer greater benefits than the original species or cultivars. You may have different feelings towards certain groups of plants than the original gardener had, or you may feel the need to enhance the environment, which was not evident in previous years. A good example of this is planting for bees and butterflies – both need help in our changing ecosystem, which in part is due to climate change.

Red admiral butterfly on *Verbena bonariensis* at Harveys Garden Plants. (Harpur Garden Images)

Bumblebee on *Eryngium bourgatii* at Harveys Garden Plants. (Harpur Garden Images)

When revamping an existing border it is usually not necessary to remove every plant. Leave some shrubs or special perennials that can quickly form the structure of the new planting. They may need pruning into shape so the growth can be more natural since the overcrowding has been removed. Depending on the time of year, the pruning may involve the sacrifice of the current year's flower buds.

Once this has been accomplished, you should then plot the existing plants on a border plan and proceed as if you were planning the plants for a new border. (*See* Chapters 5 and 6 for border plans for specific locations and soil type.)

CREATING A NEW BORDER

If you are considering creating an entirely new border, it is vital to choose your site carefully. Consider the following:

- How close to the house?
- Are there French doors or windows in close proximity? If so consider the view from inside the house.
- Will the new border lie in shade or sun? Will your favourite plants grow properly in this position?
- Are there unsightly objects or neighbours' overlooking windows that will need obscuring?

Size of the Border

How large should the border be? Obviously this

HSP summerhouse. (Harveys Garden Plants)

A SENSE OF MYSTERY

Not all of the borders should be viewed directly from the house. A strategic path that leads the eye to a curve in the path and then to a secret area within the garden adds mystery. It entices the viewer out into the garden to discover this area. Once there, they may find a gazebo, or an arbour where one can sit and enjoy a quiet moment, perhaps with refreshments. A 'coffee spot' is a favourite euphemism. These secret areas are particularly important in large gardens.

will depend on the size of the garden and the style of planting. For borders consisting of primarily shrubs, the width of the border should be a minimum of 2m and 5m long. I consider this to be the smallest necessary to accommodate three average sized shrubs and a few groupings of perennials.

Ideally shrub-only borders need to be larger to accommodate a greater range of interesting shrubs. You should match the size of the shrubs to the border to avoid excessive pruning, which ruins the natural shape of the shrub. For example, shrubs of the stature of *Ribes* 'White Icicle' should be allowed to reach its full potential (3m × 3m) rather than attempt to contain it to 1.5m × 1.5m. This will also maximize flowering. This Ribes is a delightfully scented shrub flowering in April and smelling of honey, rather than the usual scent associated with Ribes (cat pee).

Style or Type of Planting

When planning the style of border, bear in mind that shrubs and perennials look fabulous together, with shrubs forming the continuous structure and generally a brief period of flowering whilst perennials give ground cover and more colour throughout the year. A border consisting of purely shrubs is usually dull, even if variegated shrubs are used.

Shrubs mixed with tall grasses seldom look

happy. This is probably because grasses tend to have a more relaxed movement and float in the wind, which interrupts the stiffer structure of shrubs. However, grasses and perennials are natural partners in a herbaceous border. When perennials are past their best in late autumn, grasses such as *Miscanthus* species are in full regale and will provide structure through the most severe winters, even when snow has forced the collapse of the 'browns' (dead perennials that have been left over winter with their seed-heads).

Ribes 'White Icicle'. (Harpur Garden Images)

If you do fancy grasses, some smaller grasses like *Pennisetum alopecuroides* 'Hameln' or *Stipa tenuissima* can look fine at the front of a shrub and perennial border, as these grasses will tend to be planted amongst perennials.

If you decide on perennials alone, you could have smaller borders, but do avoid lots of small island beds as the effect is not restful on the eye. Island borders look far better if they are linked by arches or other suitable structures, giving them a

Grasses and perennials in high summer. (Harveys Garden Plants)

more permanent look. (*See* Chapters 5 and 6 for some suggested border plantings.)

STARTING WITH A NEW GARDEN

When starting with a new garden that does not have any borders, just a blank canvas, you need to establish how much time you will have for gardening and general maintenance. You may get over-ambitious and plant lots of borders only to find that there is not sufficient time to weed and keep the garden attractive. The garden then becomes a burden, and being in your treasured space becomes stressful.

The way forward is to consider the garden as a whole and design a plan to involve the whole garden, and then break it down into bite-size chunks that you can manage comfortably. You may decide on a series of borders in different parts of the garden; prioritize these borders and decide on maybe one or two to get started. The rest will follow on as time and funds allow.

Some of the thoughts above in creating a new

border also apply to starting a garden afresh, but here are more considerations as well.

Level or Flat?

If the garden is flat, do you have a mound of soil available to add more contrast, and possibly build a raised area?

On the other hand if the new border is to be made on a steep bank, this is a most difficult planting proposition, so you should consider terracing to create planting areas that are less steep or even flat. The most natural way to construct the terracing is with sleepers. If steps are to be made to enable people to walk to the upper levels, it is advisable to secure wire netting to the treads to avoid an accident. Unrivened wood will soon become covered in algae, and make the steps slippery, especially in winter.

SLEEPERS

Sleepers can be bought in a variety of forms, but essentially they are either new or 'used', and chemically treated or untreated. For garden use it is best to choose sleepers that have not been treated with tar or creosote, since if these treated sleepers come into contact with plant life the chemicals can leach and either severely distort plants or, in the worse scenario, actually kill them. Hard woods (oak is commonly available) generally last longer than untreated soft woods. However, new treated softwood sleepers are now available, and the treatment is kind to plants.

Pathways

Be sure to place paths appropriately, and use solid materials, such as reclaimed bricks, granite sets or paving for areas of high wear. Bark, although an organic material and of low cost, will degrade quickly. It will need topping up regularly, and will

Steep bank before terracing.
(Harveys Garden Plants)

ABOVE AND LEFT: Oak sleepers used
to terrace the steep bank. (Harveys
Garden Plants)

Terracing of steep bank.
(Harveys Garden Plants)

be 'soggy' during spells of wet weather. Well-mown grass paths always look the most attractive, but soon get muddy even with relatively little use. Gravel paths are suitable, but use a flat shingle such as Frimstone. The small stones tend to be oval and flattened. These then bind together when laid so that the shingle will not move when walked on (also highly recommended for drives).

Granite sets placed around the edge of the drive will contain gravel therein, and stop the gravel spilling out onto the road. The same can be achieved with bricks too, but do not use soft house bricks or reclaimed bricks for this purpose,

as they will disintegrate within a short period of time. It is far better to use hard engineering bricks.

Another material which has gained in popularity over recent years is the self-binding gravel called Goldpath. This is laid over hardcore, wetted and rolled flat. It settles to a hard finish, and is most suitable for paths, though not so suitable for a terraced area or patio where there are tables and chairs which are constantly pushed in and out. Hollows will appear where the gravel has been pushed aside. Obviously it can be replaced once more, but it needs to be rolled tight afterwards.

Granite sets used to contain gravel in drive. (Harveys Garden Plants)

Lawn

Ask yourself whether grass is a necessity in your garden. This question is particularly important for smaller town and shady gardens. For many gardeners a garden is not complete without a patch of grass. However in shady gardens grass is difficult to establish and maintain to a high standard. Special shady grass seed is available, but it is not vigorous and therefore will not stand hard wear. It is preferable in these situations to use another porous substrate like peashingle (gravel of 6mm or 10mm in size). A permeable membrane should be placed below the shingle so that water will drain through but stop weeds and more importantly worms from appearing at the surface.

Water

Water in the garden is relaxing, whether it is tumbling over a large rock or is a stream running through the garden. Remember that during this initial planning stage pipe-work and indeed electric cables for pumps need to be thought through.

**Water in the garden.
(Harveys Garden Plants)**

Lighting

Lighting in the garden can enhance the period of enjoyment, particularly in the autumn when days are getting shorter but the temperature may well be warm enough to sit outside until late evening.

Focus

Whether you are designing a new series of borders or a complete garden, statuary or unusual artefacts can add a touch of romance and the 'wow' factor. These surprises might include a stumpery (a collection of tree stumps stacked together) planted with ferns and hostas. Or you might create a living willow feature by planting live willow stems and weaving a structure – simple but most effective.

TOP:
Stumpery.
(Design: Rodney Burn, Surrey)

MIDDLE:
Stumpery.
(Design: Francesca Cleary, RHS Hampton Court Palace Flower Show)

BOTTOM:
Living willow structure.
(Design: Annabel Dallas, Wilts)

2 ASSESSING YOUR SITE

As part of the preparatory work before planting, you need to assess the growing conditions your site will offer the plants you choose. These considerations include the aspect (sun/shade), the type and condition of soil and the supply of water. The next stage will be to survey your garden and borders so you can draw a plan.

ASPECT

First you must determine what aspect the border lies – does the border enjoy sun, shade or semi-shade? To monitor this, take notes on the rise and fall of the sun throughout the day (in early summer ideally, as in winter when the sun is low in the sky many gardens tend to have more shade cast than in the summer). For plants, whether shrubs or perennials, it is the hot summer sun that is important to their survival. So note the position of the early morning sun (east) and then watch the progression of the sun during the day until it sets in the evening (west).

SOIL TYPE

For plants to give of their best the gardener needs to understand the nature of the soil in which the plants are to grow. Some plants prefer 'heavy' soils (clay-based), and some prefer 'light soils', which have a high content of sand.

In Suffolk I garden on heavy sticky clay soil. Suffolk gardeners refer to this as 'luvin soil', that

OPPOSITE: **Summer in the garden. (Eastgrove Cottage Garden, Worcs)**

SUN OR SHADE

Determining the aspect of your border is crucial to being able to select the correct plants and watch them grow into healthy specimens. I classify a border that is 'in full sun' as having sun from between 11am and about 3pm in the afternoon. This is generally the hottest part of the day. A shady border will have shade all day long, with perhaps the exception of early morning and late evening. Obviously these are the coolest parts of the day.

Semi-shade is an interesting term. Often referred to as dappled shade, this requires light shade to be provided by trees with small leaves, for most of the day and certainly during the hottest part of the day. Such trees often used are *Sorbus aucuparia* and cvs (rowan or commonly known as mountain ash), or *Betula species* (birch, often with interesting coloured bark, for example the river birch *Betula nigra,* with peeling red bark, and the Himalayan birch (of which there are now several cultivars) *Betula utilis* 'Jacquemontii', with peeling white bark. This looks absolutely amazing in winter especially if planted in groups. To achieve the brilliantly white stems many gardeners wash the bark in late autumn, either with a sponge and soapy water or with a pressure hose, which is particularly effective to remove green algae and dirt lodged in crevasses collected over the year. There is a magnificent display at Anglesey Abbey in Cambridgeshire (National Trust).

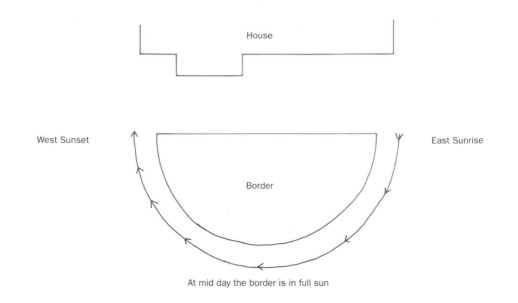

At mid day the border is in full sun

ABOVE: **South-facing border.**

BELOW: *Sorbus aucuparia.* **(Harpur Garden Images)**

is to say, the soil is wet and sticky (this can be for six months of the year). It sticks to your boots and is difficult to remove easily, hence the reference to 'luvin'. Conversely the Brecklands, which are also in Suffolk, have some of the lightest soils imaginable. Much of this land is reclaimed heath and is commonly referred to as 'Boys' Land' by those that garden on heavy soil, the inference being that you can garden on this light soil at any time of the year, and it is easy to cultivate even after heavy rains (well, perhaps after leaving an hour for the water to drain through).

However, whereas light soils are easy to work, they are inherently nutrient poor. During the normal decomposition of organic matter (humus) to its constituent nutrients, soil moisture dissolves these important components into the soil water so plants can absorb essential elements through their roots. Unfortunately on light soils these nutrients are readily washed through the soil fraction and are lost to ground water. Whereas on clay soils the nutrients are adsorbed onto the clay fraction and this makes them less vulnerable to being washed away. Clay soils are also rich in phosphate, essential for good root growth, and especially potash, essential for bountiful flowering and consequently seed production.

Lists of plants suitable for the various soil types can be found in the Appendix at the back of this book.

How to Identify your Soil

There are several categories of soil type:

- Clay loam
- Sandy clay loam
- Loam
- Fine sandy loam
- Sandy loam
- Coarse sandy loam

Sometimes soil type will vary across the garden. If this is the case, several different samples will need to be taken, as the plants that are ideal for each soil type will also vary. For example if the garden is predominantly sunny, but the soil is clay based in one corner then *Polygonatum* cultivars (Solomon's seal), roses and asters will grow well, whereas these will not grow properly on sandy soil which may occur elsewhere in the garden. In sandy soil on the other hand you would plant *Scabiosa caucasica*, *Gaura lind* and *Anthemis tinctoria*, for example.

To determine which soil type prevails in your garden, take a sample of the soil, which should be moist but not excessively wet, and perform the following tests.

Clay loams are sticky and difficult to work if wet. To identify the clay loam, roll a small portion into a ball and rub it between the thumb and index finger. If clay is present you should notice a shine on the soil, and the soil will bind well.

For sandy clay loams, follow the same procedure as above, and you should see the shiny presence of clay and also a gritty representation of sand, grit and stone. This soil is one of the most fertile, and is more workable than pure clay soils, since the sand and stone open up the soil structure.

Loam soils are characterized by their dark colour and sticky nature. If you take a sample of moist soil, it will prove difficult to make a clean ball.

Sticky particles will inevitably remain on your hands. There will also be an absence of obvious sand particles. This soil is also fertile and provides a grand medium for growing a wide range of plants, even better if there is some sand or grit in the soil. Ancient meadows that have been recently cultivated often provide highly fertile loamy soils, as the worms and other microbes that have been left undisturbed for hundreds of years have broken down copious amounts of organic matter into humous nutrients that have remained in the soil. In this soil on no account should you add extra fertilizer when planting shrubs or perennials. Growth will be vigorous and may need to be reduced during the first couple of years to avoid masses of soft growth that will lead to plants collapsing due to the abundance of available nutrients.

Fine sandy loams are extremely fertile and are often referred to as 'silts'. These soils are found near rivers or valley bottoms, where after hundreds of years the floodwaters have receded and left deposits of nutritious soil. These soils also tend to be sticky but can be identified by the shiny nature of the soil, compared to a loam. If you rub the soil between your thumb and index finger you may be able to feel some very fine sand in the sample. This soil tends to bind together better than a pure loam.

Sandy loam soils are a great growing medium, although they require more water than the above-mentioned soils, as rain will tend to flow through them more freely. These soils enable a wide range of plants to be grown. To identify a sandy loam, rub a sample of moist soil between your thumb and index finger held up to your ear. You will immediately hear a gritty noise that indicates the presence of sand. Also in the garden you will often see deposits of fine sand on the surface of the soil.

Coarse sandy loams include heath soil, where rain washes straight through to the subsoil and out of range of plant roots. Firstly, as above there will be obvious deposits of coarse sand grains on the soil surface, giving an immediate clue. Again rub a sample between your thumb and index finger held up to your ear, and you will hear the obvious gritty nature indicating the presence of sand.

Most perennials will root in the top 30cm of soil, whereas large shrubs may root down into 1m. Therefore for these shrubs it is important to consider the subsoil as well. Soils overlying chalk can present a challenge, as you may find that there is shallow layer of good topsoil and then chalk subsoil, a situation particularly prevalent in Cambridgeshire. These soils tend to be excessively dry and thus you have to treat them as if they were free draining.

Soil pH (Indicating Acidic or Alkaline Soils)

Most plants seem to tolerate a relatively wide range of soil pH if mineral nutrients are in good supply. Some plants however are particular about the soil pH in which they will grow.

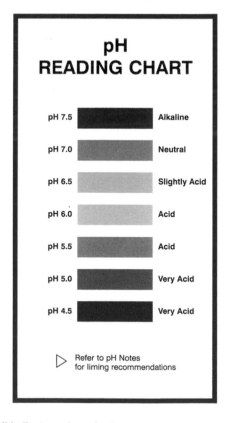

pH READING CHART

pH 7.5		Alkaline
pH 7.0		Neutral
pH 6.5		Slightly Acid
pH 6.0		Acid
pH 5.5		Acid
pH 5.0		Very Acid
pH 4.5		Very Acid

▷ Refer to pH Notes for liming recommendations

Soil indicator colour chart.

It is well known that rhododendrons and camellias require acid soil to thrive. This denotes a pH of below 7 (neutral). Usually a pH of 6 is fine, but a pH below 5 can be harmful to all but the most tolerant plants. These plants have adapted to acid soil, which is low in calcium, magnesium and potassium and high in metal ions such as iron, manganese, zinc and aluminium. While acid loving plants may be able to grow in soils that are not as acid as in their natural habitats, when grown on neutral or alkaline soils they often get iron deficient and absorb too much calcium, which disrupts their metabolism. Conversely plants that do not like acid soil are often harmed by the high levels of metal ions. Lime loving plants require a pH above 7, and ideally 8. Above this a much narrower band of plants will survive.

To assess the soil pH, you can purchase a soil testing kit from a local garden centre, or use litmus solution added to a solution of soil and barium sulphate at the correct quantities. Soil pH meters and probes are also widely available.

WATER SUPPLY

At this stage of planning it is appropriate to consider how you are going to water the border (if at all). Certainly during the first year newly planted borders will require some water during dry spells so the plants grow quickly and get established.

The choice of watering system is up to you. Hand watering may be rather a hit and miss affair, with some plants having too much water whilst others do not have enough. This leads to inter- mittent growth, and odd plants within a group looking poor, especially with regard to flowering. You will find a full range of automatic watering systems if you consult the internet. If you are considering systems with buried hose you need to decide this at an early stage and the pipes need to be laid during border preparations.

Seep hose laid out around the plants is a partic- ularly economical way to water the newly planted beds and is a system I use widely, particularly for the watering of soft fruit.

All artificial systems of watering have their drawbacks. If too much water is applied, nutrients naturally produced by the soil micro-organisms will be leached away and thus plants may show a yellowing of the leaves. This problem occurs sometimes if the watering system is left to run indiscriminately, disregarding natural rainfall. I encountered similar difficulties with a seep hose system installed for a client. The installation of a fertilizer applicator to the system, so that a measured amount of fertilizer was added to the water periodically, largely overcame the problem. A time clock can also be added to the water point so that watering can occur at night to minimize water loss due to evaporation. Many of these timers do not require an electrical supply.

Another drawback of any piped irrigation system on the surface of the soil is the unsightly nature of the pipe work. If it is buried then there is the problem of spiking the pipes with a border fork when weeding. This does not need to be a major issue if repairs are carried out immediately, as you will forget about the 'injury'. You may decide to have a temporary watering system for perhaps the first year or two. In this case the seep hose system is particularly suitable as it can be removed at any point.

One of the most inefficient methods of watering is the oscillating lawn irrigator. Not only is it extremely wasteful of the amount of water used,

thus making it environmentally unsustainable, but also it may be expensive if a water meter is installed.

Recycling rainwater is the most efficient way to water the garden. I installed a 6,000 litre tank underground – this tank was so large it needed a full size roof ladder to climb out of the hole in the ground! I was amazed how quickly it could be emptied during a drought if I was not vigilant enough about the volume of water used to irrigate the garden. If you have a large garden to irrigate consider a concrete tank to hold up to 20,000 litres of rainwater, which will be filled in winter at nil cost from the rain collected off the roof of an average four-bedroomed house. The average water-butt contains 100 litres of water, which of course is better than nothing. Several large water butts can be deployed to collect water from the house down-pipes, a garden shed and the greenhouse if required. This will be 'soft water', ideal for watering ericaceous plants.

Pests and diseases can potentially be a problem with rainwater stored in a water butt for long periods. This water should not be used to water seedlings since fungal diseases such as pithium can kill these tender and immature plants which older mature specimens would tolerate. To sterilize the water add a few crystals of potassium permanganate, which will not normally affect plants at low concentrations.

**Seep hose for irrigation.
(Harveys Garden Plants)**

3 SURVEYING THE GARDEN AND DRAWING THE PLAN

SURVEYING THE GARDEN AND BORDER

In order to produce a fully considered planting scheme, either for the garden or for individual borders, it is important to carry out a survey to include the various areas to be modified. Essentially this means measuring the garden, borders and points of interest using fixed known points. By taking measurements from several places in the garden you can accurately pinpoint the positions of key features. Usually you would draw the position of any buildings, including the house, so

that your borders can relate to these permanent structures. Remember to mark the position of windows and doors, especially French doors or similar which may be widely used in the summer.

Having completed the survey you are then ready to draw the plan.

DRAWING THE PLAN

Tools

If you are going to save funds by constructing the drawings yourself then good basic drawing tools

OPPOSITE: *Crambe cordifolia*, providing a cloud of tiny white flowers, can almost be forgiven for its pungent smell of rotting brassicas later.

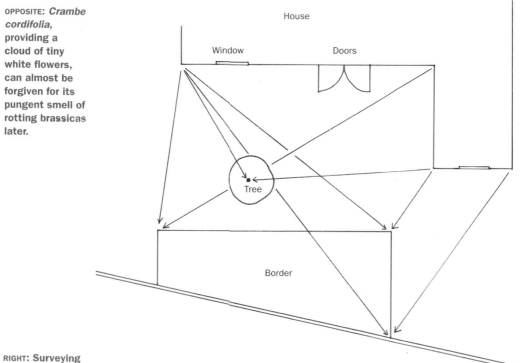

RIGHT: **Surveying the garden.**

will make the job easier and also produce good quality drawings, building confidence in the project.

Suggested drawing tools include:

A2 drawing board with prop
A2 tracing paper (100gsm)
Graph paper
Quality pencils (H and 2H)
Coloured crayons, pencils
Hard putty rubber (does not smudge)
Permanent black ink drawing pens and markers (0.5, 0.8, fine and medium)
Set square
Set of squares 45 degree angle and 60/30 degree angle
Extendable compass
Circle template
Ruler (40cm and 12cm Perspex or equivalent)
Spray paint

How to Begin

Having taken accurate measurements of the border(s), including important garden features, you should then transfer these onto paper, using a hard pencil – HB pencils are soft and wear down quickly, and also in the case of mistakes or alterations H pencil marks are easier to remove.

I use A2 tracing paper $90gm^2$, and below this I place a grid (or graph paper) which fits the particular scale I am working with. It is important to use a relatively easy scale so that you are not constantly referring back to scale tables, thus reducing the possibility for error. A drawing scale I commonly use is 1:50, that is 1.0cm on paper represents 50cm of border, or 2cm on paper represents 1.0m (100cm) of border. This is easy and practical to use.

The size A2 fits a conveniently sized drawing board which will be suitable for most desks. Also I prefer the 100gsm weight for tracing paper as you can easily make alterations without the paper ripping.

Outline drawings should be drawn in pencil first so that if you decide to change your original thoughts it is a relatively simple exercise to rub out the lines with a putty rubber and start again. The advantage of using a putty rubber is that it does not leave ugly smudge marks.

Blue line paint on grass. (Harveys Garden Plants)

You usually plot the position of the house and other outbuildings first. If you are considering borders in the back garden, for example, it may be sufficient to draw the back of the house only. This may be represented as a single line, but it is important to mark the position of the windows and doors as described above.

The next stage is to draw the perimeter of the garden.

Once you are happy with the drawing thus far, it is then a good idea to ink in these lines as a permanent feature.

If you are not sure where the borders should lie within the garden, or what shape and size is appropriate, then place another sheet of tracing paper over the first and mark the position of the house and buildings on this too. You can then experiment by drawing different shaped borders in various parts of the garden. This process can continue until you are happy with the final outcome.

At this stage it is probably a good idea to move outside and transfer your thoughts from paper to the garden itself. To do this I enlist the help of bright orange ropes reclaimed from BT – these ropes have a diameter of about 1cm and when placed on the ground can be seen from a distance. The advantage of this is that I can move the ropes to make different shaped borders, and indeed form prospective borders in different parts of the garden. Alternatively flexible water hose can also be employed to the same effect.

This should confirm your preliminary thoughts with regard to the shape and size of borders.

Once you are happy with the position and/or shape of the new borders you can spray paint the outline on the ground with a road marker. Having tried many colours over the years I have decided one of the best colours to use is blue.

Congratulations

This point I feel marks a milestone – not only have you made decisions about the size and position of the borders, but you are now able to determine the aspect of your borders and, significantly, apply due attention to the content of these new borders!

4 CHOOSING THE RIGHT PLANTS FOR THE RIGHT PLACES

It helps if you are a natural list-maker when designing a garden. In order to create a border where the 'right plant' has been put in the 'right place' it is advisable to make ample lists of the trees, shrubs and perennials that you like and which are suitable for this border.

First you need to bear in mind climate. The choice of plants that will thrive in Cornwall with its maritime environment will be quite different to those that will grow successfully in the north of England. Then you must consider the aspect, pH, and soil type. After this the plant characteristics, such as flower colour, month of flowering, height and spread, shape of leaf, evergreen or deciduous, will all need to be thought through. I find one of the best ways to do this is by constructing a spreadsheet (*see* Appendix at the back of the book).

Unfortunately there is no shortcut to the making of lists. Good plant knowledge is not essential but is obviously extremely helpful. By trolling through a range of gardening books and trusted specialist nursery catalogues you can construct an invaluable source of information that can be used time and time again.

Avoid invasive plants unless for specific difficult positions. For example *Euphorbia amygdaloides* var. *robbiae* looks attractive and inviting, but if you plant this in a fertile border, within a few years it will out-compete the other plants and fill the border by itself. It can then take several years to eradicate. There is a position where it is ideally suited and that is dry shade. This is a notoriously difficult area to plant, and not many plants can survive these harsh conditions. This euphorbia not only survives but will thrive on the poorest dry soil and dense shade. Here the tough conditions limit the plant's invasive characteristics.

Another perennial also incredibly invasive is *Euphorbia* 'Fens Ruby'. Again a lovely attractive plant in a pot, but once in the ground it runs everywhere and I doubt if anyone would ever be able to remove it all again from their garden.

RIGHT: ***Euphorbia amygdaloides** var. **robbiae**.* (Harpur Garden Images)

OPPOSITE: ***Dahlia*** 'David Howard' making an impressive display with *Rudbeckia* in the background.

Early summer at RHS Hyde Hall. (RHS Hyde Hall, Essex)

HOW TO SPOT A THUG

When purchasing plants grown in pots look at how the plant fills the pot. If there are masses of shoots emerging around the side of the pot then it is likely that this plant is going to be a thug, and best avoided in your garden. Alternatively ask a qualified person at the nursery for more details about the plant's character – you may get a surprise. You can also check out the plant on the web.

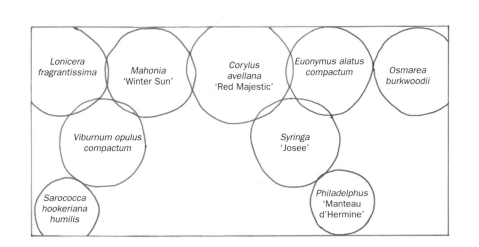

Initial placing of shrubs to give structure to the border.

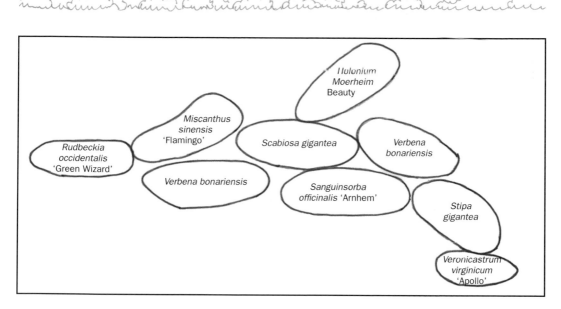

Initial placing of perennials to give structure to the border.

Visits to good gardens and nurseries with gardens will also provide you with inspiration and ideas about plant combinations that work well on those soils. Try to visit gardens with soil closely matched to one's own. Ideally most of the plants on one's list need to be easy to grow and easy to maintain.

For comprehensive lists of plants suitable for different aspects and soil types, *see* the Appendix at the back of the book.

ESTABLISHING THE STRUCTURE

When starting to decide the border content, the first objective is to decide the make-up of this border. Is it to be mixed shrubs and perennials or perennials and grasses, or just perennials? Once this has been decided consider the plants to give structure first, whether this is the taller perennials and grasses or shrubs.

A consideration to bear in mind is the proximity of any hedges. These hedges will inevitably need trimming and reshaping each year, so when planning the position of plants in front of the hedge remember to leave enough room so that you are able to cut the hedge with reasonable comfort. For example, if a shrub is expected to grow to about 2m in height and is placed in front of the hedge you should allow 80cm between the hedge front (after clipping) and the eventual edge of the plant and then about 1m to the centre of the hole to be dug for the new plant. This will enable the plant to grow to its full potential without impediment from the hedge and enable you to trim the hedge appropriately.

PERENNIALS AND GRASSES

The secret to planning a successful border with perennials only, or perennials and grasses, is to try to make it look as natural as possible. After a few years the original plants will have produced seed and these will have grown into flowering plants and be dispersed among the initial plantings,

Stipa gigantea and *Echinacea purpurea* 'Bradfield hybrids'. (Harveys Garden Plants)

giving a naturalized planting. Some seedlings will grow in inappropriate places, and may need to be removed.

You do not need to use perennials that need staking unless they happen to be particular favourites. Tall perennials with stiff stems that fulfil these characteristics include *Sanguisorba officinalis* 'Arnhem'. This grows up to 2.2m on clay soils whereby the flower stems are light and airy, topped with deep red bobbles. Another with similar characteristics includes *Scabiosa gigantea*, again growing to 2.2m with lemon yellow scabiosa flowers – perfectly hardy. Of course there is the old favourite *Verbena bonariensis*, with its wonderful purple flowers on light and airy stems. This plant will nearly always overwinter if cut down in December to 25cm from the ground. It will produce masses of seed, and if the stems are left on the plant until late December these seeds will drop around the mother plant and germinate the following spring. The seedlings will grow anywhere – between paving stones and at the base of walls to name but two sites. Another worthwhile taller plant is the bronze fennel, *Foeniculum vulgare purpurum*. Grasses that give structure

Verbena bonariensis. (Harpur Garden Images)

include *Calamagrostis* 'Overdam' and *Calamagrostis* 'Karl Foerster' with their bronze plumes during summer, *Stipa gigantea* (Golden oat) and *Miscanthus sinensis* cultivars such as 'Flamingo' growing to 2m with deep pink plumes.

When positioning these taller plants on your drawing remember that you should try to achieve a variation of height throughout the border, so that not all the talls are at the back and shorter perennials at the front – this would look contrived and unnatural. These taller perennials are light and open, which means that you can look through the stems to view plants beyond. Indeed as many of these plants seed about, it is inevitable that seedlings will occur near the front of the border, but may not look out of character as they have this light and airy feel.

In the Orchard Room border at Harveys Garden Plants, there is a predominance of taller perennials in a relatively narrow border that has been designed to great effect when viewed from inside the Orchard Room. The light and airy perennials look delightful in summer and autumn, majestically waving in the breeze.

High summer at RHS Harlow Carr. (RHS Harlow Carr, Harrogate)

Once you are happy with the plants offering structure you can then infill with your favourite other plants. The number of planting groups is important as is the number of plants in each particular group. If you plant in clumps of small numbers it looks unsettling to the eye. It is far better to plant in drifts of five, seven or more, depending on the size of the border. At my nursery, the large borders often incorporate twenty to thirty plants of a single cultivar to give impact in borders that measure up to 45m long. These are planted in waves like an artist's brush strokes, occasionally broken up with smaller groups to add a punctuation mark – a comma, which tends to lead the eye to pause, before carrying on.

DIVIDING PERENNIALS

If you already have large clumps of perennials and you can spare some of these plants to replant in the new border, you can lift these clumps and divide them into fist-sized pieces. The division is best carried out with a sharp large-bladed kitchen knife. (A brightly coloured handle will help to identify it within a heap of soil or plant debris.) Forget the traditional method of using two forks, or a spade and a fork – this is too cumbersome and brutal.

SHRUB BORDERS

Borders which are predominantly shrubs are commonly designed for people who are getting older and less able to manage the upkeep, or for people who are short of gardening time. These borders if cleverly thought through can provide year-round interest: flower colour, leaf interest and coloured winter bark all make a contribution at different times of the year. Perennials can then be added to provide groundcover, to minimize weeding.

Matching the Size to the Space

The choice of shrubs should be dependant on the space available. For example if the border is 1m wide you should not be planning to use shrubs that have a spread of 2m or more, as these plants will encroach onto the surface surrounding the border. This is especially a problem if grass is edging the border. The overhanging shrub will kill the grass and when you decide to reduce the overall size of the shrub, an ugly patch of earth will be exposed.

If the border is positioned in front of a fence, and you wish to hide the fence, then the width of the border needs to be appropriate. For example: You have a 2m fence to hide. Most shrubs that grow to 2m will also have a spread of the same. Therefore the width of the border should be at least 2m. *Philadelphus* 'Belle Etoile' and *Philadel-*

Large bladed kitchen knife, and a clump of *Veronica gentianoides* before division. (Harveys Garden Plants)

Clump of *Veronica gentianoides* after division. (Harpur Garden Images)

Mixed border of shrubs and perennials. (RHS Hyde Hall, Essex)

phus 'Beauclerke' both grow to about 2m in good fertile soil with a spread of the same. Wonderful shrubs, flowering in June, the former has single white flowers with a maroon throat and the latter single white flowers with some pink shading around the stamens, both are highly scented of orange and therefore a must for all shrub borders. They grow in sun or semi-shade, which makes these shrubs versatile.

Another reason for using shrubs that are the correct size for the given space is to minimize pruning. For example: if you are trying to contain a stunning shrub like *Kolkwitzia amabilis* (the Beauty Bush), which has an arching, spreading habit, growing to 3m in height and spread, with light brown flaky bark, by heavy pruning you will inevitably ruin the shape and waste your time with extra work in doing so. This rather defeats the principle of a labour-saving border.

If the border has to be limited in size in front of a fence, so that the height of the fence far exceeds the width of the border, then climbers should be considered to clothe the fence. The choice of climber is important to compliment the planting in front. Aspect also has to be considered. *Lonicera* cultivars are good for a shady spot,

THINK IN MULTIPLES

Sometimes it is appropriate to plant shrubs in groups and not as singles, especially in large dramatic landscapes that involve extensive borders. Single planted shrubs will usually take a minimum of five years to make a worthwhile specimen, whereas five or even seven large shrubs planted as a drift will give real impact quickly. Alternatively three shrubs planted close together (about 70cm apart and in the shape of a triangle) will grow as one and fill a gap much quicker than a single shrub.

Philadelphus 'Belle Etoile'. (Harpur Garden Images)

Wire supports for climbers. (Harveys Garden Plants)

whereas clematis and rose species and cultivars, with careful consideration, can be chosen for any aspect.

If you have to clothe a wooden fence I would recommend that a series of wires be attached to the fence posts using vine eyes. This provides an inconspicuous way of providing support for climbers, and also allows air to circulate behind the stems and leaves of the climber, reducing disease pressure.

Kolkwitzia amabilis. (Harpur Garden Images)

ALWAYS HAVE A PLAN B

Some years back the team and I were planting a client's garden. There were two borders to plant. When the first border was finished I turned my attention to the second border, but where was the plan? After wandering around this rather large garden I found it, unhappily in a myriad of small pieces. The owner's dog had found it a useful plaything. It was impossible to put the plan back together, so I had to revert to my memory. The moral of the story is to always take a copy of the plan – at least you will have a back-up.

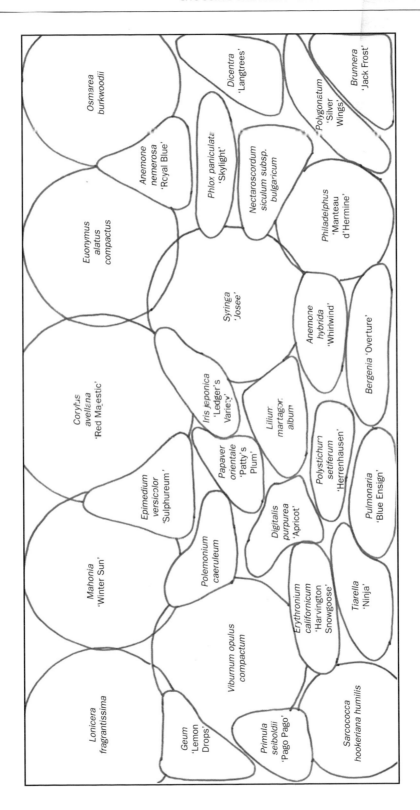

Shrubs and perennials for a large semi-shady border with loam soil – 32m2 (8×4m).

PLANTS	NUMBER
Shrubs	
Corylus avellana 'Red Majestic'	1
Euonymus alatus compactum	1
Lonicera fragrantissima	1
Mahonia 'Winter Sun'	1
Osmarea burkwoodii	1
Philadelphus 'Manteau d'Hermine'	1
Sarcococca hookeriana humilis	1
Syringa 'Josee'	1
Viburnum opulus compactum	1
Perennials	
Anemone hybrida 'Whirlwind'	5
Anemone nemerosa 'Royal Blue'	9
Bergenia 'Overture'	7
Brunnera 'Jack Frost'	5
Dicentra 'Langtrees'	7
Digitalis purpurea 'Apricot'	5
Epimedium versicolor 'Sulphureum'	9
Erythronium californicum 'Harvington Snowgoose'	9
Geum 'Lemon Drops'	5
Iris japonica 'Ledger's Variety'	5
Lilium martagon album	7
Nectaroscordum siculum subsp. *bulgaricum*	7
Papaver orientale 'Patty's Plum'	5
Phlox paniculata 'Skylight'	7
Polemonium caeruleum	7
Polygonatum 'Silver Wings'	7
Polystichum setiferum 'Herrenhausen'	5
Primula seiboldii 'Pago Pago'	7
Pulmonaria 'Blue Ensign'	5
Tiarella 'Ninja'	7

ABOVE: *Dicentra* 'Langtrees'. (Harpur Garden Images)

ABOVE: *Sarcococca hookeriana humilis.* (Harpur Garden Images

BELOW: *Corylus avellana* 'Red Majestic'.

Bergenia 'Overture'. (Cotswold Garden Flowers)

Tiarella 'Ninja'.
(Cotswold
Garden Flowers)

Mahonia 'Winter Sun'. (Harpur Garden
Images)

Syringa 'Josee'. (Harpur Garden Images

BOTTOM LEFT:
Anemone hybrida
'Whirlwind'. (Harpur
Garden Images)

BOTTOM RIGHT: *Brunnera* 'Jack
Frost'. (Cotswold Garden
Flowers)

5 BORDER PLANS FOR PERENNIALS

We've already looked at how to draw border plans, and how to select plants to fill one's drawing. This is a time-consuming process, and you may not have the time or the inclination to carry out this process to its conclusion, so this chapter and the one following contain twenty-five examples of border plans for the various aspects encountered – shade, semi-shade and sun. The border plans offered are further subdivided into soil type.

For example, if you have a border that is approximately 4m × 2m; is shady, has a soil pH of about 7, and the soil is clay or loam, then look no further than the first plan. This indicates the choice plants and numbers required to fill this area. The illustration is of a perfect rectangle. Of course it is likely the border will be more irregular, but the principle will remain the same, and the number of plants will remain the same, provided the area of the border is similar – in this case 8m².

The accompanying table suggests using five or seven of the same plants, rather than three. This is deliberate as the border will look more restful to the eye, compared with a larger number of smaller groups.

A frequently asked question concerns which plants to grow in dry soils under trees. The answer to this is that all soils will dry out during prolonged periods without rain. The important point to consider is the nature of the soil, whether it is sandy or clay based. Plants grown in clay based soils are better able to withstand drought, as microscopic water particles adhere to clay grains and thus the fine roots of plants can absorb these water particles as the soils dry out. Sandy soils have no microscopic reserves of water and thus in arid times the plants dry out much quicker on these soils – hence the need to identify the soil type correctly, as discussed in Chapter 2.

Epimedium versicolor **'Neosulphureum'. (Harpur Garden Images)**

OPPOSITE: One frosty day. (Harveys Garden Plants)

SHADY TOLERANT PERENNIALS

In Clay and Loam Soils

Small Border
The plants chosen for this border will all grow on 'stronger' soils and tolerate shade. The *Geranium phaeum* family are very versatile plants; not only will they tolerate a wide range of soils in shade, but will reflower if all the foliage and flowers are removed after flowering. This action removes diseased foliage (mildew), which may build up if

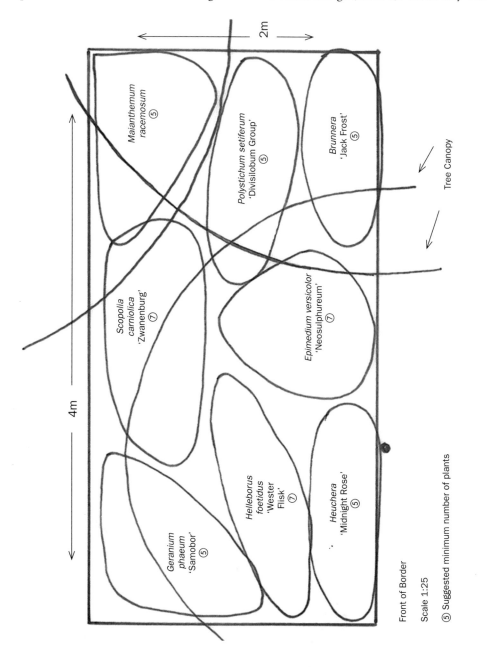

Shade tolerant perennials for a small clay and loam soil border, 8m² (4 × 2m).

Front of Border

Scale 1:25

⑤ Suggested minimum number of plants

PLANTS	NUMBER
Geranium phaeum 'Samobor'	5
Helleborus foetidus 'Wester Flisk'	7
Heuchera 'Midnight Rose'	5
Scopolia carniolica 'Zwanenburg'	7
Epimedium versicolor 'Neosulphureum'	5
Maianthemum racemosum	5
Polystichum setiferum 'Divisilobum Group'	5
Brunnera 'Jack Frost'	5

the plant is stressed due to drought. *Helleborus foetidus* 'Wester Flisk' is a relative of our native *Helleborus foetidus* (stinking hellebore), which can be found growing abundantly in the woodlands of East Anglia. *Scopolia carniolica* 'Zwanenburg' is a native to Eastern Europe (Romania and Hungary) and, although poisonous, has attractive red tubular flowers on a self-supporting stem growing to about 80cm. Heuchera cultivars are a versatile group of plants with evergreen foliage, which is often coloured.

Polystichum setiferum 'Divisilobum Group'. (Cotswold Garden Flowers)

Medium Border

In this diagram I have suggested some garden trees that will offer dappled shade. The planting of these trees should be no closer to a building than the mature height of the tree. *Amelanchier* 'Robin Hill' will grow to between 5–10m tall, therefore the planting distance from a house should be not less than 9–10m. This is a beautiful tree with a dense, oval habit. It produces masses of spring flowers that open pink and turn white.

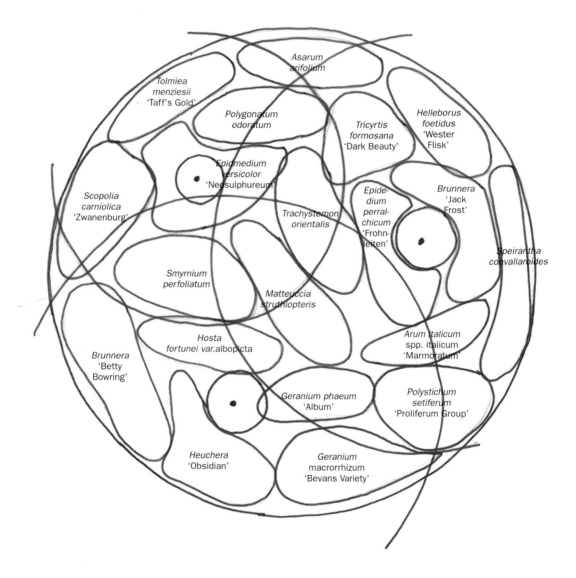

Shade tolerant perennials for medium clay and loam soil border, 20m².

LEFT: *Asarum arifolium.* (Harper Garden Images)

RIGHT: *Scopolia carniolica* 'Zwanenburg'. (Harper Garden Images)

This North American selection has coppery-red young leaves that harden to green by late spring, before they turn a vivid red in autumn. Other easy plants include *Polygonatum odoratum*, a scented form of Solomon's seal that is less prone to sawfly; the cultivar *Brunnera* 'Betty Bowring' with pure white flowers which will lighten a dark spot and Jack Frost with attractive silver marbled leaves and pale blue flowers. *Geranium macrorrhizum* is a useful species and the paler colours for shade are highly recommended. Try *Geranium macrorrhizum* 'Ingwersens Variety', which has pale pink flowers over evergreen geranium scented leaves, or *Geranium macrorrhizum album* with its almost white flowers.

RIGHT: *Smyrnium perfoliatum.* (Cotswold Garden Flowers)

Epimedium perralchicum 'Frohnleiten'. ('Harpur Garden Images)

Arum italicum spp. italicum 'Marmoratum'. (Harpur Garden Images)

Polygonatum odoratum. (Harpur Garden Images)

PLANTS	NUMBER
Trees	
1. *Amelanchier* 'Robin Hill'	1
2. *Sorbus vilmorinii*	1
3. *Betula utilis* 'Jacquemontii'	1
Perennials	
Asarum arifolium	7
Polygonatum odoratum	5
Tolmiea menziesii 'Taff's Gold'	7
Epimedium versicolor 'Neosulphureum'	11
Scopolia carniolica 'Zwanenburg'	7
Matteuccia struthiopteris	7
Smyrnium perfoliatum	9
Hosta fortunei var. *albopicta*	7
Brunnera 'Betty Bowring'	7
Heuchera 'Obsidian'	7
Geranium phaeum 'Album'	5
Geranium macrorrhizum	7
Polystichum setiferum 'Proliferum Group'	5
Arum italicum spp. italicum 'Marmoratum'	7
Trachystemon orientalis	5
Tricyrtis formosana 'Dark Beauty'	7
Helleborus foetidus 'Wester Flisk'	7
Brunnera 'Jack Frost'	5
Speirantha convallaroides	9
Epimedium perralchicum 'Frohnleiten'	9

Large Border

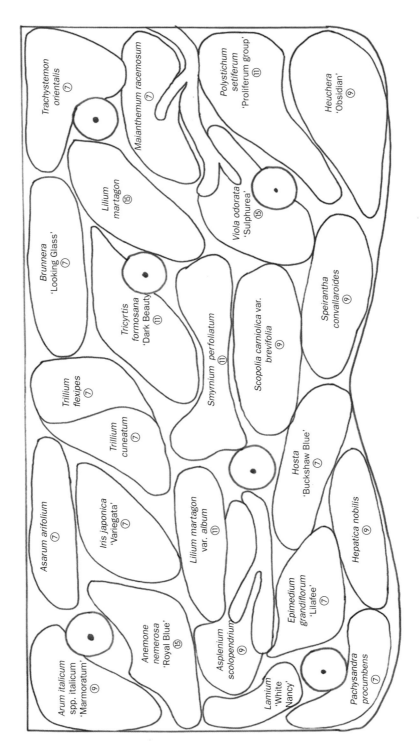

Shade tolerant perennials for large heavy clay and loam soil border, 32m² (8m × 4m).

Acer campestre is a native, more commonly known as field maple, appearing in mixed hedgerows. It is a small tree, growing to 10–15m tall, and was widely used in the Middle Ages to make musical instruments. In autumn the leaves turn yellow, red and golden brown. It casts dappled shade and so is ideal for underplanting.

Arum italicum spp. Italicum 'Marmoratum' is an interesting plant, with marbled foliage in late winter that dies down in summer and has a spike of red berries in the autumn. *Pachysandra procumbens* is a little known plant that is clump-forming, evergreen and produces short spikes of curiously spice scented white flowers in April. It is also tolerant of extremely dry soils.

It is commonly thought that hostas require damp soils to thrive; this is not the case. Most cultivars are tolerant of dry soils, except for the largest forms, and will give months of interest owing to their coloured foliage.

Epimedium grandiflorum 'Lilafee'. (Harpur Garden Images)

Iris japonica 'Variegata'. (Harpur Garden Images)

Trillium cuneatum. (Harpur Garden Images)

Brunnera 'Looking Glass'. (Cotswold Garden Flowers)

Asplenium scolopendrium. (Harpur Garden Images)

PLANTS	NUMBER
Trees	
Acer campestre (native field maple)	3
Betula pendula (native birch)	3
Perennials	
Arum italicum spp. italicum 'Marmoratum'	7
Anemone nemerosa 'Royal Blue'	9
Asplenium scolopendrium	9
Lamium 'White Nancy'	5
Epimedium grandiflorum 'Lilafee'	7
Pachysandra procumbens	7
Hepatica nobilis	9
Hosta 'Buckshaw Blue'	7
Lilium martagon var. *album*	11
Iris japonica 'Variegata'	7
Trillium cuneatum	7
Trillium flexipes	7
Brunnera 'Looking Glass'	7
Tricyrtis formosana 'Dark Beauty'	11
Smyrnium perfoliatum	11
Scopolia carniolica var. *brevifolia*	9
Speirantha convallaroides	9
Viola odorata 'Sulphurea'	11
Lilium martagon	11
Trachystemon orientalis	7
Maianthemum racemosum	7
Polystichum setiferum 'Proliferum group'	11
Heuchera 'Obsidian'	9
Asarum arifolium	7

In Sandy Soils

Small Border

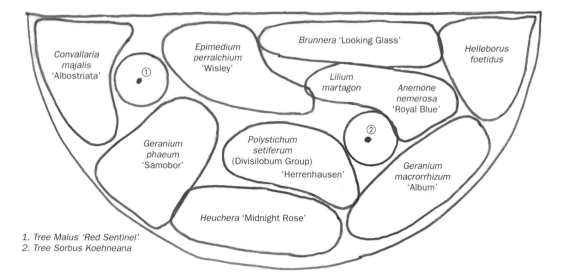

1. Tree Malus 'Red Sentinel'
2. Tree Sorbus Koehneana

Convallaria
majalis
'Albostriata'

①

Epimedium
perralchium
'Wisley'

Brunnera 'Looking Glass'

Helleborus
foetidus

Lilium
martagon

Anemone
nemerosa
'Royal Blue'

②

Geranium
phaeum
'Samobor'

Polystichum
setiferum
(Divisilobum Group)
'Herrenhausen'

Geranium
macrorrhizum
'Album'

Heuchera 'Midnight Rose'

Shade tolerant perennials for small sandy soil border 8m² (4 × 2m).

LEFT: *Polystichum setiferum* (Divisilobum Group)
'Herrenhausen'. (Harpur Garden Images)

BELOW: **Convallaria majalis 'Albostriata'. (Cotswold
Garden Flowers)**

PERENNIALS	NUMBER
Convallaria majalis 'Albostriata'	7
Geranium phaeum 'Samobor'	7
Epimedium perralchium 'Wisley'	9
Heuchera 'Midnight Rose'	5
Polystichum setiferum 'Herrenhausen'	7
Brunnera 'Looking Glass'	5
Lilium martagon	9
Anemone nemerosa 'Royal Blue'	9
Geranium macrorrhizum 'Album'	7
Helleborus foetidus	5

Shady conditions combined with sandy soil present a particularly challenging planting opportunity, generally called 'Dry Shade'. However, there are some plants that will tolerate these specialized conditions. Some epimediums will even thrive under these conditions, such as *Epimedium versicolour sulphurum* and *Epimedium perralchium* 'Wisley'. Both flower in March and April, the former with lemon yellow flowers and the latter with buttercup yellow flowers over glossy evergreen foliage. To maximize the beauty of these plants, it is advisable to remove all the foliage in early February to allow the fresh new leaves and flowers emerge. To avoid frost damage on the delicate young foliage and flowers, it is suggested not to plant epimediums in an east-facing border and avoid early morning sun striking these plants after a night frost.

Polystichum setiferum ferns are also tolerant of dry conditions, and there is a wide range of cultivars of different sizes to suit a range of growing positions.

Geranium macrorrhizum 'Album'. (Harpur Garden Images)

Medium Border

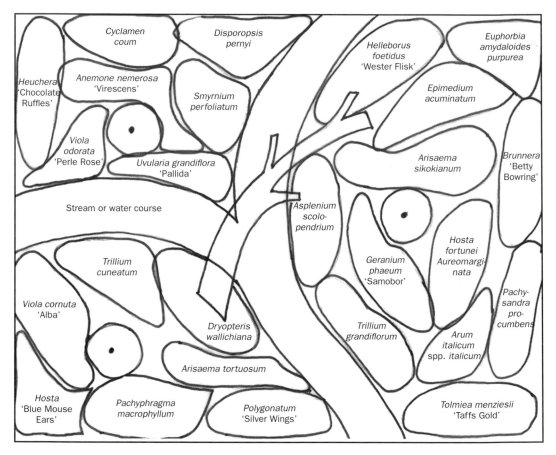

Cyclamen coum

Disporopsis pernyi

Helleborus foetidus 'Wester Flisk'

Euphorbia amydaloides purpurea

Heuchera 'Chocolate Ruffles'

Anemone nemerosa 'Virescens'

Smyrnium perfoliatum

Epimedium acuminatum

Viola odorata 'Perle Rose'

Uvularia grandiflora 'Pallida'

Arisaema sikokianum

Brunnera 'Betty Bowring'

Stream or water course

Asplenium scolo-pendrium

Hosta fortunei Aureomargi-nata

Trillium cuneatum

Geranium phaeum 'Samobor'

Viola cornuta 'Alba'

Dryopteris wallichiana

Trillium grandiflorum

Arum italicum spp. italicum

Pachy-sandra pro-cumbens

Arisaema tortuosum

Hosta 'Blue Mouse Ears'

Pachyphragma macrophyllum

Polygonatum 'Silver Wings'

Tolmiea menziesii 'Taffs Gold'

Shade tolerant perennials for sandy soil medium border 20m² (5 × 4m). Trillium and Dryopteris, although requiring damp soil, will grow alongside a stream regardless of soil type.

Epimedium acuminatum. **(Harpur Garden Images)**

Trillium grandiflorum. (Harpur Garden Images)

Euphorbia amygdaloides 'Purpurea'. (Harpur Garden Images)

Our native wood anemone grows and spreads to form huge carpets in deciduous woodlands. In cultivation there is a considerable range of coloured forms, such as *Anemone nemerosa* 'Royal Blue' with deep blue flowers, *Anemone nemerosa* 'Allenii' with pale blue flowers and *Anemone nemerosa* 'Picos Pink' with pale pink flowers. These all flower in spring and die down in the summer, only to reappear in late winter.

Disporopsis pernyi is an evergreen relative of our native *Polygonatum hybridum* (Solomon's Seal). It does suffer from sawfly, but has scented white drooping flowers in May–June, and is tolerant of extremely dry conditions.

Our native Harts Tongue Fern *Asplenium scolopendrium* can often be found growing in rock crevices in walls, as well as other dry places, and so will grow easily in dry conditions under trees.

Cyclamen coum and *hederifolium* are both hardy, even though they originate from the Mediterranean. The former flowers from January to March, the latter from August to October. Do not be tempted to plant mixed colonies, as *Cyclamen hederifolium* will out-compete *Cyclamen coum*. Both seed prodigiously, and form large colonies in time.

Geranium phaeum 'Samobor'. (Harpur Garden Images)

Heuchera 'Chocolate Ruffles'. (Cotswold Garden Flowers)

Pachysandra procumbens. (Harpur Garden Images)

PERENNIALS	NUMBER
Heuchera 'Chocolate Ruffles'	7
Viola pensylvanica 'Perle Rose'	9
Anemone nemerosa 'Virescens'	9
Cyclamen coum	9
Disporopsis pernyi	7
Smyrnium perfoliatum	7
Uvularia grandiflora 'Pallida'	7
Viola cornuta 'Alba'	9
Hosta 'Blue Mouse Ears'	5
Trillium cuneatum	7
Dryopteris wallichiana	7
Arisaema tortuosum	5
Polygonatum 'Silver Wings'	5
Helleborus foetidus 'Wester Flisk'	7
Epimedium acuminatum	9
Euphorbia amygdaloides 'Purpurea'	5
Arisaema sikokianum	9
Asplenium scolopendrium	7
Hosta fortunei Aureomarginata	7
Pachysandra procumbens	9
Trillium grandiflorum	7
Arum italicum spp. italicum 'Marmoratum'	7
Brunnera 'Betty Bowring'	7
Tolmiea menziesii 'Taffs Gold'	7
Pachyphragma macrophyllum	7
Geranium phaeum 'Samobor'	7

SEMI-SHADE TOLERANT PERENNIALS

In Heavy Clay Soils

Small Border

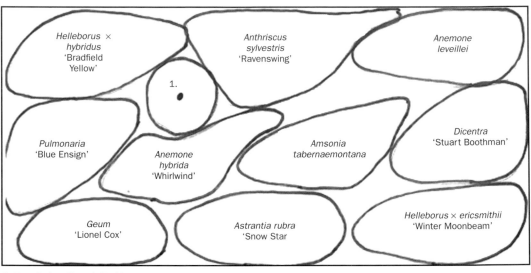

*Helleborus ×
hybridus
'Bradfield
Yellow'*

*Anthriscus
sylvestris
'Ravenswing'*

*Anemone
leveillei*

1.

*Pulmonaria
'Blue Ensign'*

*Anemone
hybrida
'Whirlwind'*

*Amsonia
tabernaemontana*

*Dicentra
'Stuart Boothman'*

*Geum
'Lionel Cox'*

*Astrantia rubra
'Snow Star'*

*Helleborus × ericsmithii
'Winter Moonbeam'*

1. Tree *Sorbus* 'Joseph Rock'

Semi-shade tolerant perennials for small, heavy clay soil border 8m2 (4m × 2m).

LEFT: **Dicentra 'Stuart
Boothman'. (Harpur Garden
Images)**

RIGHT: **Anthriscus sylvestris
'Ravenswing'. (Harpur Garden
Images)**

Helleborus hybridus 'Bradfield Yellow'. (Harpur Garden Images)

Anemone leveillei. (Harpur Garden Images)

Semi-shade offers growing conditions that enable a greater range of plants to thrive and flower compared to full shade, as more light is available to the growing plants. Often sunlight will penetrate the tree canopy for short periods of time, and generally not at mid-day which is the hottest part of the day in summer. Semi-shade borders are not always shaded by trees. Tall buildings and houses will also cast shade, particularly in cities, but light levels will generally be greater than under trees, so the choice of plants should be categorized as those needing semi-shade.

Helleborus hybridus Bradfield hybrids are a wonderful group of plants found in a range of colours and make marvellous characters for semi-shade and retentive soils (e.g. clay based). They typically flower from January to April. It is suggested to plant lighter colours in dark places,

PERENNIALS	NUMBER
Helleborus hybridus 'Bradfield Yellow'	5
Pulmonaria 'Blue Ensign'	5
Anthriscus sylvestris 'Ravenswing'	5
Anemone hybrida 'Whirlwind'	7
Geum 'Lionel Cox'	5
Astrantia rubra 'Snow Star'	7
Amsonia tabernaemontana	7
Anemone leveillei	5
Dicentra 'Stuart Boothman'	7
Helleborus × *ericsmithii* 'Winter Moonbeam'	5

to brighten up these dull corners. Darker colours should be planted near to the house so that one can easily view the flowers in winter, when the flower colour is similar to the surrounding brown earth. To keep the plants in good health it is recommended that all the leaves should be removed in November. This stops any fungal spores, especially blackspot, transferring onto the new growth as it appears in January.

Anthriscus sylvestris 'Ravenswing' is a relative of our native cow parsley. It has chocolate foliage and cream flowers on stout stems in late spring. Seedlings will be produced readily, sometimes with green leaves. These are easily weeded to leave a colony with bronze foliage.

ABOVE: *Pulmonaria* 'Blue Ensign'. (Cotswold Garden Flowers)

LEFT: *Helleborus* × *ericsmithii* 'Winter Moonbeam'. (Harpur Garden Images)

Medium Border

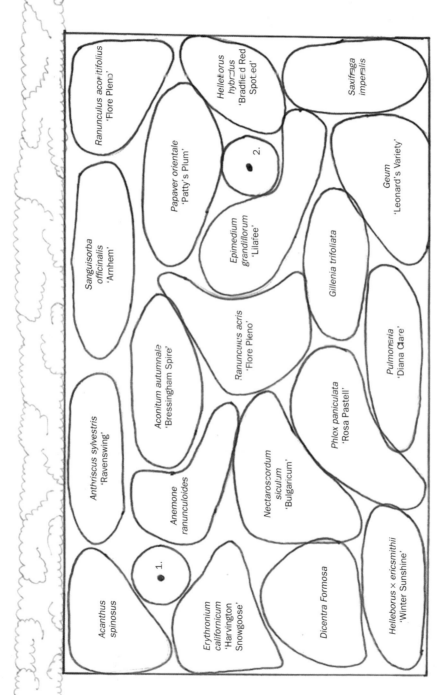

1. Tree *Acer Campestre* (Field Maple)
2. Tree *Betula Pendula* (Common Silver Birch) can be purchased as a multi stem

Semi-shade tolerant perennials for heavy clay soil medium border 20m2 (6 × 3.3m).

Labels within the plan:

- Ranunculus aconitifolius 'Flore Pleno'
- Helleborus hybridus 'Bradfield Red Spotted'
- Saxifraga imperialis
- Papaver orientale 'Patty's Plum'
- Geum 'Leonard's Variety'
- Sanguisorba officinalis 'Arnhem'
- Epimedium grandiflorum 'Lilafee'
- Gillenia trifoliata
- Pulmonaria 'Diana Clare'
- Anthriscus sylvestris 'Ravenswing'
- Aconitum autumnale 'Bressingham Spire'
- Ranunculus acris 'Flore Pleno'
- Phlox paniculata 'Rosa Pastell'
- Anemone ranunculoides
- Nectaroscordum siculum 'Bulgaricum'
- Acanthus spinosus
- Erythronium californicum 'Harvington Snowgoose'
- Dicentra Formosa
- Helleborus × ericsmithii 'Winter Sunshine'

Erythronium californicum 'Harvington Snowgoose'. (Harpur Garden Images)

Helleborus × *ericsmithii* 'Winter Sunshine'.

Nectaroscordum siculum 'Bulgaricum'. (Harpur Garden Images)

Papaver orientale 'Patty's Plum'. (Cotswold Garden Flowers)

Some Acanthus species are tolerant of semi-shade (*Acanthus spinosus* and *Acanthus mollis*), while others, such as *Acanthus hirsutus*, will only thrive in full sun. The flowering of the former two species will not be as prolific in semi-shade as in full sun, but they can make useful groundcover. The white and lavender flower spikes are large and dramatic, with lovely seed-pods showing large bronze seeds in the autumn. However, be aware that once these plants are grown in a particular area they are difficult to remove as they have an extensive tap root. A systemic herbicide containing glyphosate is the only effective method.

Erythroniums (dog tooth violets and trout lilies) are easy to grow in clay-based or loam soils, provided the soil is enriched with compost and manure. The flower colour varies from violet (*dens canis* cultivars) with attractive marbled leaves to pure white (*E. californicum* 'Harvington Snowgoose') and lilac-pink (*E.* 'Harvington Wild Salmon'). *Erythronium dens canis* cultivars ('Old Aberdeen' is one of the best) grow to about 15cm, whilst *Erythronium californicum* 'Harvington Snowgoose' grows to about 25cm tall. All flower in March and April and no suitable border should be without them.

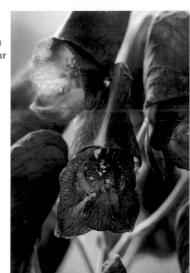

Aconitum autumnale 'Bressingham Spire'. (Harpur Garden Images)

BELOW: *Dicentra Formosa.* (Cotswold Garden Flowers)

LEFT: *Acanthus spinosus.* (Harpur Garden Images)

RIGHT: *Helleborus hybridus* 'Bradfield Red Speckled'. (Harpur Garden Images)

PERENNIALS	NUMBER
Acanthus spinosus	5
Anthriscus sylvestris 'Ravenswing'	7
Anemone ranunculoides	9
Erythronium californicum 'Harvington Snowgoose'	7
Dicentra formosa	7
Helleborus x ericsmithii 'Winter Sunshine'	5
Nectaroscordum siculum 'Bulgaricum'	9
Phlox paniculata 'Rosa Pastell'	7
Aconitum autumnale 'Bressingham Spire'	7
Pulmonaria 'Diana Clare'	7
Gillenia trifoliata	7
Ranunculus acris 'Flore Pleno'	7
Sanguisorba officinalis 'Arnhem'	7
Ranunculus aconitifolius 'Flore Pleno'	5
Papaver orientale 'Patty's Plum'	7
Epimedium grandiflorum 'Lilafee'	9
Geum 'Leonard's Variety'	7
Saxifraga imperalis	7
Helleborus hybridus 'Bradfield Red Speckled'	5

LEFT: *Pulmonaria* 'Diana Clare'. (Cotswold Garden Flowers)

RIGHT: *Ranunculus acris* 'Flore Pleno'. (Harpur Garden Images)

Large Border

For extensive planting in semi-shade, it is wise to use tough plants that give good ground cover. This will help stop weeds establishing and make the job of weeding these borders less onerous.

Euphorbias are best known as sun-loving plants for dry conditions; however, *Euphorbia grithiffii* and the cultivar 'Dixter' will grow well in shade, provided they have rich soil in which to grow. *Euphorbia grithiffii* 'Dixter' is a particular favour-ite with chestnut-tan stems and leaves. Fiery red bracts appear in May and last until September, when they become more mellow.

Pulmonarias also grow well in semi-shade. The colours range from the vivid blue *Pulmonaria* 'Blue Ensign' to the muted pinks and mauves of *Pulmonaria* 'Opal'; the red cultivar, *Pulmonaria* 'Bowles Red', and the exquisite *Pulmonaria* 'Sissinghurst White', with pure white flowers over white spotted leaves, are also recommended.

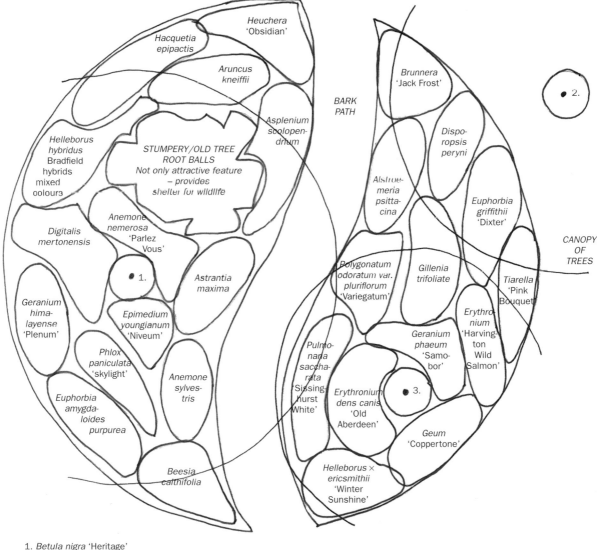

1. *Betula nigra* 'Heritage'
2. *Castanea sativa* (sweet chestnut)
3. *Sorbus scalaris*

Semi-shade tolerant perennials for heavy clay soil large border, 32m².

ABOVE: *Helleborus hybridus* Bradfield hybrids mixed colours. (Harpur Garden Images)

RIGHT: *Hacquetia epipactis.* (Harpur Garden Images)

Astrantia maxima. (Harpur Garden Images)

Gillenia trifoliate. (Cotswold Garden Flowers)

Anemone nemerosa 'Parlez Vous'. (Harpur Garden Images)

Disporopsis pernyi. (Harpur Garden Images)

Erythronium 'Harvington Wild Salmon'. (Harpur Garden Images)

Tiarella 'Pink Bouquet'. (Cotswold Garden Flowers)

Beesia calthifolia. (Harpur Garden Images)

PLANTS	NUMBER
Trees	
1. *Betula nigra* 'Heritage'	1
2. *Castanea sativa* (sweet chestnut)	1
3. *Sorbus scalaris*	1
Perennials	
Brunnera 'Jack Frost'	5
Alstroemeria psittacina	7
Disporopsis pernyi	7
Euphorbia griffithii 'Dixter'	7
Tiarella 'Pink Bouquet'	5
Gillenia trifoliate	9
Polygonatum odoratum var. pluriflorum 'Variegatum'	7
Geranium phaeum 'Samobor'	7
Erythronium 'Harvington Wild Salmon'	9
Pulmonaria saccharata 'Sissinghurst White'	7
Erythronium dens canis 'Old Aberdeen'	9
Helleborus × *ericsmithii* 'Winter Sunshine'	7
Geum 'Coppertone'	7
Heuchera 'Obsidian'	5
Hacquetia epipactis	7
Aruncus kneiffeii	5
Asplenium scolopendrium	7
Helleborus hybridus Bradfield hybrids mixed colours	5
Digitalis mertonensis	7
Anemone nemerosa 'Parlez Vous'	9
Astrantia maxima	7
Epimedium youngianum 'Niveum'	7
Geranium himalayense 'Plenum'	7
Phlox paniculata 'Skylight'	7
Anemone sylvestris	7
Beesia calthifolia	7
Euphorbia amygdaloides purpurea	7

In Sandy Soils

Small Border

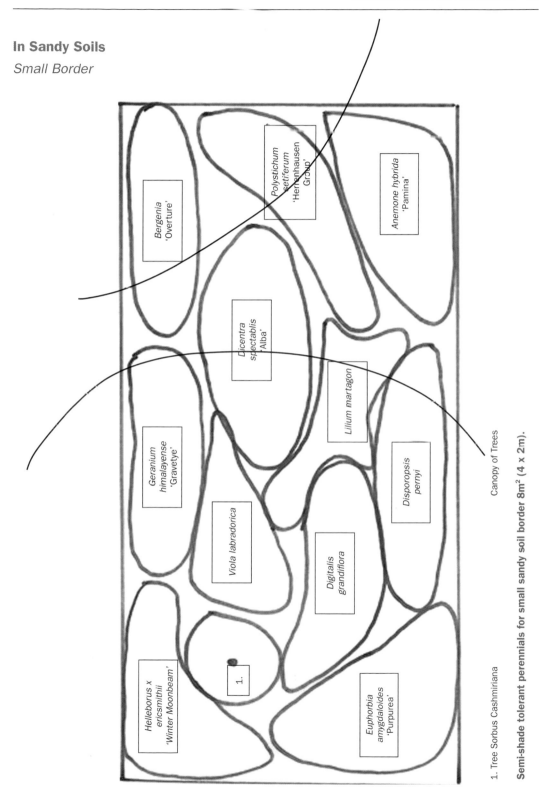

Bergenia 'Overture'

Polystichum setiferum 'Herrenhausen Group'

Anemone hybrida 'Pamina'

Dicentra spectablis 'Alba'

Lilium martagon

Geranium himalayense 'Gravetye'

Disporopsis pernyi

Viola labradorica

Digitalis grandiflora

Helleborus x ericsmithii 'Winter Moonbeam'

1.

Euphorbia amygdaloides 'Purpurea'

Canopy of Trees

1. Tree Sorbus Cashmiriana

Semi-shade tolerant perennials for small sandy soil border 8m² (4 x 2m).

PERENNIALS	NUMBER
Helleborus ×*ericsmithii* 'Winter Moonbeam'	3
Euphorbia amygdaloides 'Purpurea'	5
Digitalis grandiflora	7
Viola labradorica	9
Geranium himalayense 'Gravetye'	7
Dicentra spectablis 'Alba'	5
Bergenia 'Overture'	7
Polystichum setiferum 'Herrenhausen Group'	7
Anemone hybrida 'Pamina'	7
Lilium martagon	9
Disporopsis pernyi	7

As with shady borders, sandy soils in this category can present extremely dry conditions. Only the toughest plants will survive. Some of the most resistant plants include *Euphorbia amygdaloides* 'Purpurea', a clump-forming perennial, with typically deep purple red foliage and acid green flowers in March. These plants will seed about lightly to increase your original planting.

Anthriscus sylvestris 'Ravenswing' and *Silene fimbriata* also tolerate semi-shade when grown on sandy soils. Both will grow to 100cm and add some useful height to the border. *Silene fimbriata* has white campion flowers and interesting seed-heads after flowering.

Another taller plant is *Dicentra spectablis* and *Dicentra spectablis* 'Alba' (pink and white bleeding heart respectively). These plants start flowering in April and continue flowering until mid-May, and are quite at home in dappled shade.

Anemone hybrida 'Pamina'. (Harpur Garden Images)

Medium Border

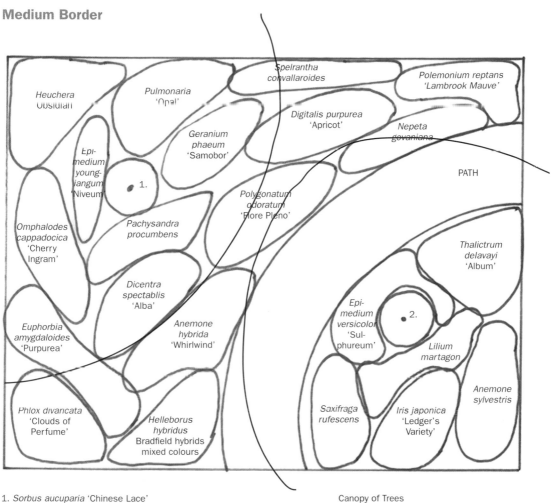

Heuchera
'Obsidian'

Pulmonaria
'Opal'

Spelrantha
convallaroides

Polemonium reptans
'Lambrook Mauve'

Digitalis purpurea
'Apricot'

Nepeta
govaniana

Geranium
phaeum
'Samobor'

Epi-
medium
young-
ianum
'Niveum

1.

PATH

Polygonatum
odoratum
'Flore Pleno'

Omphalodes
cappadocica
'Cherry
Ingram'

Pachysandra
procumbens

Thalictrum
delavayi
'Album'

Dicentra
spectablis
'Alba'

Epi-
medium
versicolor
'Sul-
phureum'

2.

Euphorbia
amygdaloides
'Purpurea'

Anemone
hybrida
'Whirlwind'

Lilium
martagon

Anemone
sylvestris

Phlox divaricata
'Clouds of
Perfume'

Helleborus
hybridus
Bradfield hybrids
mixed colours

Saxifraga
rufescens

Iris japonica
'Ledger's
Variety'

1. *Sorbus aucuparia* 'Chinese Lace'
2. *Prunus* 'Okame'

Canopy of Trees

Semi-shade tolerant perennials for medium sandy soil border 20m² (5 × 4m).

Heuchera **'Obsidian'. (Cotswold Garden Flowers)**

The species *Sorbus aucuparia* is an adaptable tree that will grow in a wide range of soils. They tend to be medium-sized trees, which offer dappled shade, flower in spring and have berries in the autumn. This is often accompanied by good autumn colour.

Turks-cap lilies (*Lilium martagon*) thrive in sandy soils enriched with leafmould or compost. They grow to 2m with alternate flowers astride a stout stem. *Lilium martagon* grows in an extensive range across Europe. The wild form has purple spotted flowers, while there are white forms (*Lilium martagon album*) in cultivation. There are numerous new hybrids in exotic colours. These plants will seed about (not invasively) to form extensive colonies,

Phlox divaricata cultivars are low growing and with flowers that have muted colours and are mostly perfumed. They flower in May and are delightful for the front of a shady border. *Phlox divaricata* 'Clouds of Perfume' is one such variety.

Anemone sylvestris. (Harpur Garden Images)

ABOVE: *Pulmonaria* 'Opal'. (Cotswold Garden Flowers)

RIGHT: *Omphalodes cappadocica* 'Cherry Ingram'. (Cotswold Garden Flowers)

Thalictrum delaveyi 'Album'. (Cotswold Garden Flowers)

Speirantha convallaroides. (Harpur Garden Images)

Lilium martagon. (Cotswold Garden Flowers)

PLANTS	NUMBER
Trees	
1. *Sorbus aucuparia* 'Chinese Lace'	1
2. *Prunus* 'Okame'	1
Perennials	
Heuchera 'Obsidian'	7
Epimedium youngianum 'Niveum'	7
Omphalodes cappadocica 'Cherry Ingram'	7
Euphorbia amygdaloides 'Purpurea'	9
Phlox divaricata 'Clouds of Perfume'	7
Helleborus hybridus Bradfield hybrids mixed colours	5
Anemone hybrida 'Whirlwind'	7
Dicentra spectablis 'Alba'	5
Pachysandra procumbens	7
Geranium phaeum 'Samobor'	5
Pulmonaria 'Opal'	7
Polygonatum odoratum 'Flore Pleno'	7
Digitalis purpurea 'Apricot'	5
Speirantha convallaroides	7
Nepeta govaniana	7
Polemonium reptans 'Lambrook Mauve'	7
Thalictrum delavayi 'Album'	7
Epimedium versicolor 'Sulphureum'	9
Saxifraga rufescens	7
Iris japonica 'Ledger's Variety'	7
Anemone sylvestris	7
Lilium martagon	9

SUN LOVING PERENNIALS
In Heavy Clay Soils

Small Border

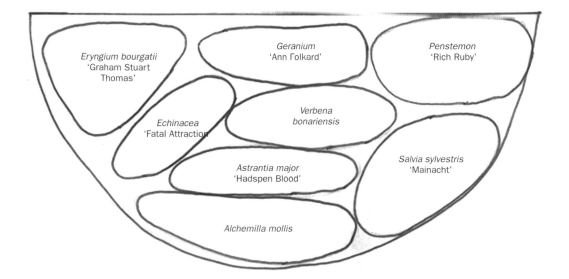

Sun loving perennials for small heavy clay soil border, 8m².

Geranium 'Ann Folkard'. (Cotswold Garden Flowers)

Eryngium bourgatii 'Graham Stuart Thomas'. (Cotswold Garden Flowers)

Echinacea 'Fatal Attraction'. (Cotswold Garden Flowers)

Sun loving perennials generally present a different range of plants to those that will grow best in semi-shade. However, there are surprisingly many plants that will grow in both semi-shade or sun. Good research will help one identify these. Planting associations for a sunny border in strong clay soils and thin sandy soils are covered in the following plans.

On clay soils it is advisable not to add fertilizer if one is planting perennials, as this will lead to the plants growing excessively and toppling over. The plants suggested in the following diagrams should not require staking, unless the soil is extremely fertile. If plants are growing too tall it is possible to reduce the overall height by cutting the plant

ABOVE: *Astrantia major* 'Hadspen Blood' (Cotswold Garden Flowers)

LEFT: *Salvia sylvestris* 'Mainacht' (Cotswold Garden Flowers)

stems by one half mid-way through the growing season. For example, with *Helenium* cultivars you can reduce the flowering height by 25cm by halving the growth in June. This effectively eliminates the leading flower buds (apical dominance), and promotes branching lower down the plant. This produces a bushier plant, a delay in flowering of about two weeks, and a plant less likely to topple over. Sedums can also be transformed in the same way.

PERENNIALS	NUMBER
Eryngium bourgatii 'Graham Stuart Thomas'	7
Echinacea 'Fatal Attraction'	7
Geranium 'Ann Folkard'	5
Verbena bonariensis	7
Astrantia major 'Hadspen Blood'	7
Alchemilla mollis	7
Salvia sylvestris 'Mainacht'	9
Penstemon 'Rich Ruby'	5

Medium Border

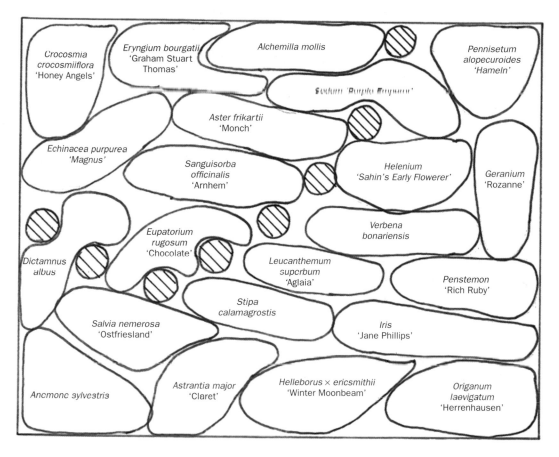

Crocosmia crocosmiiflora 'Honey Angels'

Eryngium bourgatii 'Graham Stuart Thomas'

Alchemilla mollis

Pennisetum alopecuroides 'Hameln'

Sedum 'Purple Emperor'

Aster frikartii 'Monch'

Echinacea purpurea 'Magnus'

Sanguisorba officinalis 'Arnhem'

Helenium 'Sahin's Early Flowerer'

Geranium 'Rozanne'

Dictamnus albus

Eupatorium rugosum 'Chocolate'

Verbena bonariensis

Leucanthemum superbum 'Aglaia'

Penstemon 'Rich Ruby'

Stipa calamagrostis

Salvia nemerosa 'Ostfriesland'

Iris 'Jane Phillips'

Anemone sylvestris

Astrantia major 'Claret'

Helleborus × ericsmithii 'Winter Moonbeam'

Origanum laevigatum 'Herrenhausen'

Sun loving perennials for medium heavy clay soil border, 20m².

***Crocosmia crocosmiiflora* 'Honey Angels'.
(Cotswold Garden Flowers)**

Clay-based soils provide ideal growing conditions for a wide range of summer and autumn flowering perennials because they hold reserves of water for longer periods than lighter, sandy soils. There-

Eupatorium rugosum 'Chocolate'. (Harpur Garden Images)

Echinacea purpurea 'Magnus'. (Harpur Garden Images)

Geranium 'Rozanne'. (Cotswold Garden Flowers)

Salvia nemerosa 'Ostfriesland'. (Harpur Garden Images)

Leucanthemum superbum 'Aglaia'. (Cotswold Garden Flowers)

Helleborus × *ericsmithii* 'Winter Moonbeam'. (Harpur Garden Images)

fore the plants typically hold onto their lower leaves for longer, thereby reducing their premature death and the ensuing brown leaves. This is typical of Asters – a lovely group of plants flowering from August (*Aster frikartii* 'Monch' with blue flowers) until November (*Aster horizontalis* 'Prince', dark foliage and pink sprays of flowers).

Helenium 'Sahin's Early Flowerer'. (Harpur Garden Images)

Aster frikartii 'Monch'. (Cotswold Garden Flowers)

PERENNIALS	NUMBER
Crocosmia crocosmiiflora 'Honey Angels'	7
Eryngium bourgatii 'Graham Stuart Thomas'	9
Echinacea purpurea 'Magnus'	7
Aster frikartii 'Monch'	5
Alchemilla mollis	5
Sedum 'Purple Emperor'	7
Sanguisorba officinalis 'Arnhem'	7
Eupatorium rugosum 'Chocolate'	7
Dictamnus albus	7
Salvia nemerosa 'Ostfriesland'	9
Astrantia major 'Claret'	7
Stipa calamagrostis	5
Leucanthemum superbum 'Aglaia'	5
Verbena bonariensis	7
Helenium 'Sahin's Early Flowerer'	7
Pennisetum alopecuroides 'Hameln'	7
Geranium 'Rozanne'	5
Penstemon 'Rich Ruby'	5
Iris 'Jane Phillips'	7
Origanum laevigatum 'Herrenhausen'	7
Anemone sylvestris	7
Helleborus × *ericsmithii* 'Winter Moonbeam'	5

Echinacea purpurea cultivars (cone flowers) are wonderful summer-flowering perennials, with rich ruby-mauve flowers; all requiring full sun and rich soils. For clay soils, you would need to add copious amounts of organic matter to make the soil more friable and ideal for these plants.

Penstemons are a versatile group of 'sub shrubs' that will tolerate a wide range of soils. They start flowering in July and carry on until November. Most are hardy, except those with wide leaves compared to 'the norm'. For example, Penstemon Blackbird has 2cm wide leaves and is not fully hardy. To improve the over-winter hardiness it is advisable to delay cutting back the foliage until the end of March. This will protect the plant during periods of severe frost.

Large Border

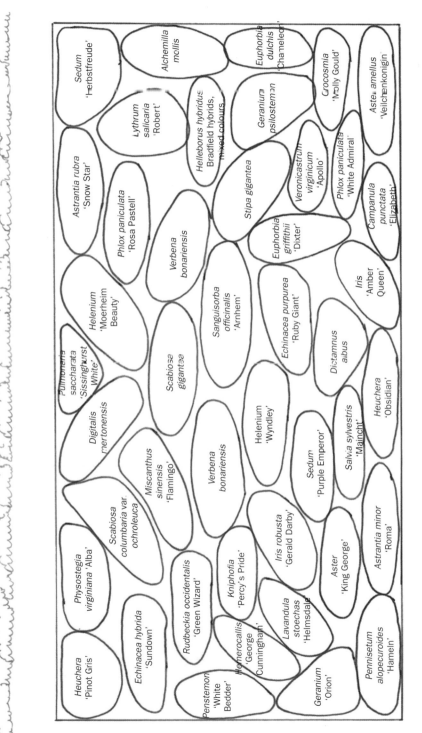

Sun loving perennials and grasses for large heavy clay soil border, 32m².

Astrantia minor 'Roma'.
(Harpur Garden Images)

Grasses can make an important contribution to a perennial border. *Stipa gigantea* (Golden Oat) is impressive as it flowers in June, and holds its seed-heads until mid-winter. It combines well with *Geranium psilostemon* or *Geranium* 'Patricia'. Both have bright magenta flowers with a black eye, and flower all summer.

Another group of impressive grasses is the Miscanthus, which flower in September. *Miscanthus sinensis* 'Flamingo' with its soft pink stems and plumes of flowers is particularly impressive. The seedheads hold all through the winter, and look particularly impressive with frosts highlighting the cobwebs.

Sanguisorba officinalis 'Arnhem' is a wonderful tall floaty perennial reaching 2m. The delightful spring foliage is keenly sought after by flower arrangers. In summer, tall stout stems hold aloft sprays of small deep-red bobble heads. It will also tolerate semi-shade.

Rudbeckia occidentalis 'Green Wizard' is absolutely fabulous. It grows to 120cm with black domed cones and gold flecks. Bumble bees love it.

Sedums are so important, both from an environmental point of view and to enhance the autumn vibrancy. Bees and butterflies smother sedums in the autumn, as they provide a rich source of nectar, which is in short supply at this time of the year. Various cultivars are available from *Sedum* 'Purple Emperor' with dark foliage and deep red flowers to *Sedum* 'Iceberg' with white flowers. Perhaps a variety to avoid is *Sedum* 'Frosty Morn'; variegated foliage and clashing pink flowers!

Echinacea hybrida 'Sundown'. (Harpur Garden Images)

Heuchera 'Pinot Gris'. (Cotswold Garden Flowers)

Aster 'King George'. (Cotswold Garden Flowers)

Hemerocallis 'George Cunningham'. (Harpur Garden Images)

Helleborus hybridus Bradfield hybrids, mixed colours. (Harpur Garden Images)

Echinacea purpurea 'Ruby Giant'. (Cotswold Garden Flowers)

Euphorbia griffithii 'Dixter'. (Cotswold Garden Flowers)

PERENNIALS	NUMBER
Heuchera 'Pinot Gris'	5
Physostegia virginiana 'Alba'	7
Echinacea hybrida 'Sundown'	7
Rudbeckia occidentalis 'Green Wizard'	7
Kniphofia 'Percy's Pride'	5
Iris robusta 'Gerald Darby'	7
Sedum 'Purple Emperor'	7
Salvia sylvestris 'Mainacht'	7
Heuchera 'Obsidian'	5
Astrantia minor 'Roma'	7
Aster 'King George'.	7
Lavandula stoechas 'Helmsdale'	7
Hemerocallis 'George Cunningham'	5
Penstemon 'White Bedder'	5
Geranium 'Orion'	5
Pennisetum alopecuroides 'Hameln'	7
Scabiosa columbaria var. *ochroleuca*	7
Digitalis mertonensis	7
Pulmonaria saccharata 'Sissinghurst White'	5
Helenium 'Moerheim Beauty'	7
Astrantia rubra 'Snow Star'	7
Sedum 'Herbstfreude'	5
Alchemilla mollis	5
Phlox paniculata 'Rosa Pastell'	7
Scabiosa gigantea	5
Miscanthus sisnensis 'Flamingo'	5
Helenium 'Wyndley'	7
Dictamnus albus	5
Iris 'Amber Queen'	7
Echinacea purpurea 'Ruby Giant'	7
Sanguisorba officinalis 'Arnhem'	7
Euphorbia griffithii 'Dixter'	7
Stipa gigantea	5

Veronicastrum virginicum 'Apollo'	5
Phlox paniculata 'White Admiral'	7
Aster amellus 'Veilchenkonigin'	7
Geranium psilostemon	5
Euphorbia dulcis 'Chameleon'	7
Helleborus hybridus Bradfield hybrids, mixed colours	5
Lythrum salicifolia 'Robert'	7
Campanula punctata 'Elizabeth'	5
Verbena bonariensis	7

Sedum 'Purple Emperor'. (Harpur Garden Images)

Phlox paniculata 'White Admiral'. (Harpur Garden Images)

Helenium 'Moerheim Beauty'. (Harveys Garden Plants)

In Sandy Soils

Small Border

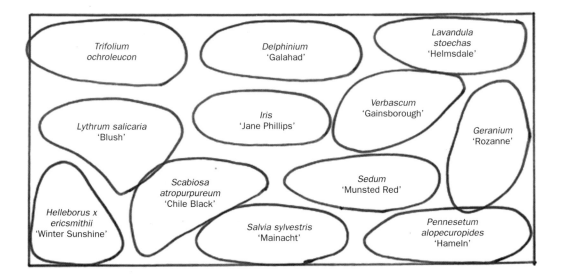

Sun loving perennials and grasses for small sandy soil border, 8m2 (4 × 2m).

PERENNIALS	NUMBER
Trifolium ochroleucon	7
Delphinium 'Galahad'	7
Lavandula stoechas 'Helmsdale'	7
Verbascum 'Gainsborough'	7
Geranium 'Rozanne'	5
Pennesetum alopecuropides 'Hameln'	7
Sedum 'Munsted Red'	7
Salvia sylvestris 'Mainacht'	7
Iris 'Jane Phillips'	7
Lythrum salicaria 'Blush'	7
Scabiosa atropurpureum 'Chile Black'	7
Helleborus × ericsmithii 'Winter Sunshine'	5

This is a more difficult growing environment, since if plants are stressed due to lack of water the flower buds may wither and never flower. The foliage will be disappointing as the plant struggles to survive. However, a select band of plants has overcome these difficulties and forms the basis of the plants selected for the diagrams below. These are typically Mediterranean plants or cultivars of plants thriving in these harsh conditions. For example, the plants often have silver or grey leaves to reflect the sun, and small narrow leaves to minimize water loss. Lavender, sage, thyme, rosemary and oreganum are all good examples.

Trifolium ochroleucon is a stunning plant, easy to grow and flowers in June and early July. The large cream clover-shaped heads never cease to attract attention. Bees love this plant too.

Trifolium ochroleucon.
(Harpur Garden Images)

Medium Border

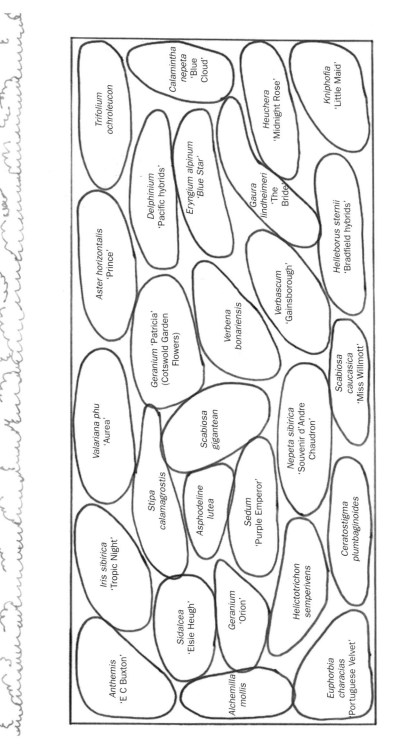

Sun loving perennials and grasses for medium sandy soil border, 20m² (6 × 3.3m).

Agapanthus cultivars grow particularly well in dry sandy conditions. The species *Agapanthus africanus* grows wild in South Africa, but is not hardy in the UK except in Cornwall and the Isles of Scilly. Elsewhere it is best grown in pots and removed to a greenhouse with frost protection during the winter. The narrow-leaved forms are completely hardy when planted in the ground, with Agapanthus headborne hybrids and *Agapanthus* 'Black Pantha' having withstood frosts to -17C in 2011 and daytime temperatures of -8C. The key point to ensure good flowering is full sun. These plants need to be baked in summer.

Eryngiums (sea hollies) are particularly suitable for hot dry conditions. Recommended cultivars include *E. bourgattii* 'Graham Stuart Thomas', with its silvered leaves and dark blue flowers, *Eryngium alpinum* 'Blue Star', with feathery tactile large blue flowers, and *Eryngium oliverianum*, with its crisp spikes of deep blue flowers.

Geranium 'Patricia'. (Cotswold Garden Flowers)

Kniphofia 'Little Maid'. (Cotswold Garden Flowers)

PERENNIALS	NUMBER
Anthemis 'E C Buxton'	7
Iris siberica 'Tropic Night'	7
Valariana phu 'Aurea'	5
Aster horizontalis 'Prince'	7
Trifolium ochroleucron	7
Sidalcea 'Elsie Heugh'	5
Stipa calamagrostis	5
Asphodeline lutea	5
Scabiosa gigantean	5
Sedum 'Purple Emperor'	7
Nepeta sibirica 'Souvenir d'Andre Chaudron'	7
Scabiosa caucasica 'Miss Willmott'	7
Ceratostigma plumbaginoides	7
Euphorbia characias 'Portuguese Velvet'	7
Helictotrichon semperivens	5
Geranium 'Orion'	5
Alchemilla mollis	5
Geranium 'Patricia'	5
Delphinium 'Pacific hybrids'	7
Eryngium alpinum 'Blue Star'	7
Calamintha nepeta 'Blue Cloud'	5
Verbena bonariensis	7
Verbascum 'Gainsborough'	5
Gaura lindheimeri 'The Bride'	7
Helleborus sternii 'Bradfield hybrids'	5
Kniphofia 'Little Maid'	7
Heuchera 'Midnight Rose'	7

WRONG PLACE?

Don't worry about 'mistakes'. Most plants are robust and you can certainly move them after the first growing season without any harm. Perennials can be moved most successfully in late September and up to mid October. They then have an opportunity to re-root into relatively warm soils. For evergreen shrubs this is best carried out in early October, and for deciduous shrubs in early November after the leaves have dropped.

PERENNIAL BORDERS TO
ATTRACT BEES AND BUTTERFLIES

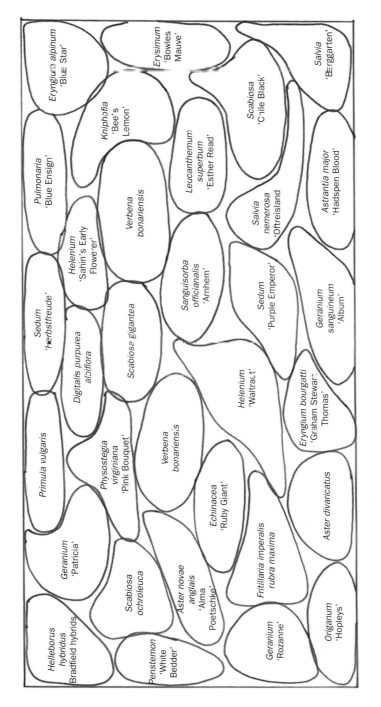

Perennials to attract bees and butterflies.

As our climate changes all gardeners are being encouraged to consider wildlife, and especially to plant for bees and butterflies. The Appendix at the back of the book contains an extensive list of perennials that bees and butterflies find attractive. These plants are mostly sun lovers, but early flowering plants such as hellebores and snowdrops provide valuable nectar for early foraging bees. These can be planted in full sun among other perennials, providing the soil is loam or clay based. Single flowers provide nectar for the foraging insects, whereas double flowers do not or only produce small amounts; it is usually the nectaries that have enlarged to form another layer of petals or sepals. Therefore avoid planting double flowered plants if the aim is to attract bees and butterflies.

To encourage plants to produce good supplies of nectar it is important to keep the plants in good health and water regularly during periods of drought. Bees also require water to produce honey in the hive. There are many annuals that are attractive to bees, especially the later flowering borage. It is reputed that bees will travel miles to seek this herb. Borage will self-seed in the border, so further planting should be unnecessary.

ABOVE: *Helenium* 'Sahin's Early Flowerer'. (Harpur Garden Images)

BELOW: *Helleborus hybridus* Bradfield hybrids (Picotee). (Harpur Garden Images)

Helenium 'Waltraut'. (Harpur Garden Images)

PERENNIALS	NUMBER
Aster divaricartus	7
Aster novae anglais 'Alma Poetschke'	7
Astrantia major 'Hadspen Blood'	9
Digitalis purpurea albiflora	9
Echinacea 'Ruby Giant'	7
Eryngium alpinum 'Blue Star'	7
Eryngium bourgatti 'Graham Stewart Thomas'	7
Erysimum 'Bowles Mauve'	7
Fritillaria imperalis rubra maxima	11
Geranium 'Patricia'	7
Geranium 'Rozanne'	5
Geranium sanguineum 'Album'	7
Helenium 'Sahin's Early Flowerer'	7
Helenium 'Waltraut'	7
Helleborus hybridus Bradfield hybrids (Picotee)	5
Kniphofia 'Bee's Lemon'	9
Leucanthemum superbum 'Esther Read'	5
Origanum 'Hopleys'	7
Penstemon 'White Bedder'	5
Physostegia virginiana 'Pink Bouquet'	9
Primula vulgaris	9
Pulmonaria 'Blue Ensign'	7
Salvia 'Berggarten'	5
Salvia nemerosa 'Oftreisland'	9
Sanguisorba officianalis 'Arnhem'	7
Scabiosa 'Chile Black'	7
Scabiosa gigantea	7
Scabiosa ochroleuca	7
Sedum 'Purple Emperor'	7
Sedum 'Herbstfreude'	7
Verbena bonariensis	14

6 BORDER PLANS FOR MIXED SHRUBS AND PERENNIALS

Borders that are full of both shrubs and perennials provide colour throughout the year, without the need to replant annual bedding plants every year.

In the winter garden shrubs come into their own, and plans are offered here for mixed borders that will be satisfying as well as labour-saving.

OPPOSITE: Shrubs with coloured foliage, such as *Physocarpus opulifolius* 'Diabolo' create a useful foil for the perennials in the foreground.

BELOW: *Geum* 'Lionel Cox' (in lower left corner). (Harpur Garden Images)

YEAR-ROUND INTEREST
Sun Loving Plants in Loam Soil

Medium Border

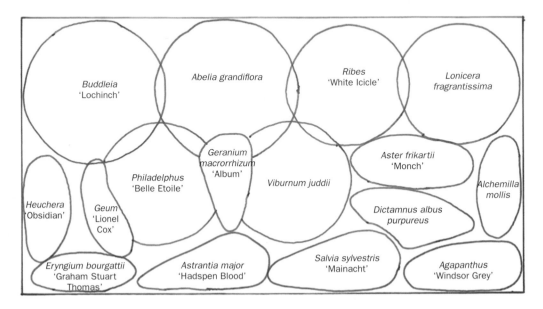

Sun loving shrubs and perennials for year-round interest in a medium loam soil border, 20m² (6 × 3.3m).

Abelia grandiflora. (Harpur Garden Images)

Ribes 'White Icicle'. (Harpur Garden Images)

A sunny border offers the greatest range of shrubs for year-round colour. The choice of shrubs needs careful consideration so that the eventual size matches the space available. For example, if the space available is 2m width, it is not advisable to plant a shrub that will attain 3–4m when mature. It is generally accepted that the mature height of a shrub should be based on the growth after five years. In this situation it would be fine to plant *Abelia grandiflora* (2m^2) but not *Kolkwitzia amabilis* (3.5m^2).

There are so many beautiful shrubs from which to choose, it is tempting to plant too many in any given space. This may offer a flavour of several; but each plant is unable to show off its characteristics majestically, and thus the planting becomes a hedge. Alternatively you may be tempted by a particular favourite, with the thought that you can keep it pruned. Usually pruning occurs at an incorrect time, so the shrub does not flower well, if at all, or the gardener prunes the shrub into an unnatural shape.

Viburnum juddii. (Harpur Garden Images)

Agapanthus 'Windsor Grey'.
(Cotswold Garden Flowers)

PLANTS	NUMBER
Shrubs	
Abelia grandiflora	1
Buddleia 'Lochinch'	1
Lonicera fragrantissima	1
Philadelphus 'Belle Etoile'	1
Ribes 'White Icicle'	1
Viburnum juddii	1
Perennials	
Agapanthus 'Windsor Grey'	7
Alchemilla mollis	7
Aster frikartii 'Monch'	7
Astrantia major 'Hadspen Blood'	7
Dictamnus albus purpureus	9
Eryngium bourgattii 'Graham Stuart Thomas'	7
Geranium macrorrhizum 'Album'	7
Geum 'Lionel Cox'	5
Heuchera 'Obsidian'	5
Salvia sylvestris 'Mainacht'	7

Astrantia major 'Hadspen Blood'.
(Harpur Garden Images)

Large Border

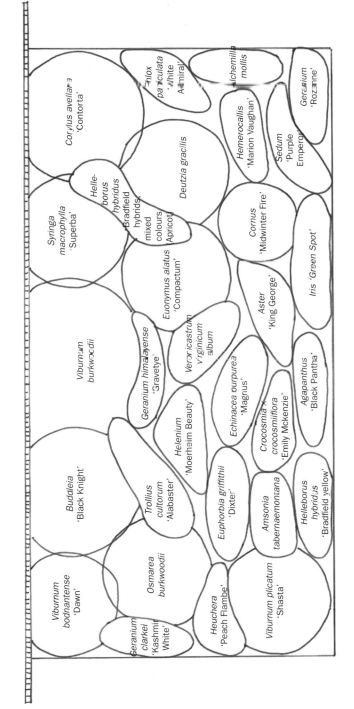

Sun loving shrubs and perennials for year-round interest in a large loam soil border, 32m² (8 × 4m).

With a large border, one may use impressive shrubs that will fill a space quickly and create impact. If the area to be planted is extensive then plant the shrubs in multiples of three, five, etc. as one would perennials. This leads to quick establishment, and thus creating impact sooner than planting single specimens.

Cornus and Salix species and cultivars feature in every garden for winter interest, but should also feature in a border for year-round interest too, as the colourful stems in winter brighten up a dreary landscape. *Cornus* 'Midwinter Fire' is a particular favourite with its amber stems topped with a fiery glow. Viburnums are splendid as the scent is so intoxicating. They come in a range of sizes, from the smallest *Viburnum juddii* (1.4m) to the taller *Viburnum carlcephalum* and *Viburnum burkwoodii*, both capable of reaching over 4m.

Trollius cultorum 'Alabaster'. (Cotswold Garden Flowers)

Helleborus hybridus Bradfield hybrids, mixed colours (Apricot). (Harpur Garden Images)

Agapanthus 'Black Pantha'. (Cotswold Garden Flowers)

Heuchera 'Peach Flambe'. (Cotswold Garden Flowers)

Amsonia tabernaemontana. (Harpur Garden Images)

Cornus 'Mldwinter Fire'. (Harpur Garden Images)

Corylus avellana 'Contorta'. (Harpur Garden Images)

Veronicastrum virginicum album. (Harpur Garden Images)

Crocosmia × *crocosmiiflora* 'Emily Mckenzie'. (Harpur Garden Images)

PLANTS	NUMBER
Shrubs	
Buddleia 'Black Knight'	1
Cornus 'Midwinter Fire'	1
Corylus avellana 'Contorta'	1
Deutzia gracilis	1
Euonymus alatus 'Compactum'	1
Osmarea burkwoodii	1
Syringa macrophylla 'Superba'	1
Viburnum bodnantense 'Dawn'	1
Viburnum burkwoodii	1
Viburnum plicatum 'Shasta'	1
Perennials	
Agapanthus 'Black Pantha'	7
Alchemilla mollis	5
Amsonia tabernaemontana	7
Aster 'King George'	7
Crocosmia × *crocosmiiflora* 'Emily Mckenzie'	9
Echinacea purpurea 'Magnus'	7
Euphorbia griffithii 'Dixter'	7
Geranium 'Rozanne'	5
Geranium clarkei 'Kashmir White'	5
Geranium himalayense 'Gravetye'	7
Helenium 'Moerheim Beauty'	7
Helleborus hybridus Bradfield hybrids, mixed colours (Apricot)	7
Helleborus hybridus 'Bradfield yellow'	5
Hemerocallis 'Marion Vaughan'	5
Heuchera 'Peach Flambe'	5
Iris 'Green Spot'	9
Phlox paniculata 'White Admiral'	7
Sedum 'Purple Emperor'	7
Trollius cultorum 'Alabaster'	9
Veronicastrum virginicum album	7

WINTER INTEREST
In Loam Soil

Medium Border

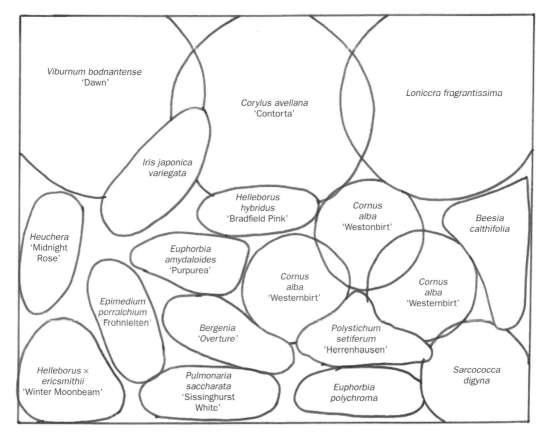

Viburnum bodnantense
'Dawn'

Corylus avellana
'Contorta'

Lonicera fragrantissima

Iris japonica variegata

Helleborus hybridus
'Bradfield Pink'

Cornus alba
'Westonbirt'

Beesia calthifolia

Heuchera
'Midnight Rose'

Euphorbia amydaloides
'Purpurea'

Cornus alba
'Westernbirt'

Cornus alba
'Westernbirt'

Epimedium perralchium
'Frohnlelten'

Bergenia
'Overture'

Polystichum setiferum
'Herrenhausen'

Helleborus ×
ericsmithii
'Winter Moonbeam'

Pulmonaria saccharata
'Sissinghurst White'

Euphorbia polychroma

Sarcococca digyna

Shrubs and perennials for a winter interest in a medium loam soil border, 20m² (5 x 4m).

Viburnum bodnantense 'Dawn'. (Harpur Garden Images)

PLANTS	NUMBER
Shrubs	
Viburnum bodnantense 'Dawn'	1
Corylus avellana 'Contorta'	1
Lonicera fragrantissima	1
Cornus alba 'Westonbirt'	1
Sarcococca digyna	1
Perennials	
Beesia calthifolia	7
Iris japonica variegata	7
Heuchera 'Midnight Rose'	5
Helleborus x ericsmithii 'Winter Moonbeam'	5
Epimedium perralchium 'Frohnleiten'	7
Pulmonaria saccharata 'Sissinghurst White'	7
Bergenia 'Overture'	7
Euphorbia amydaloides 'Purpurea'	7
Helleborus hybridus 'Bradfield Pink'	5
Polystichum setiferum 'Herrenhausen'	7
Euphorbia polychroma	5

Cornus and *Salix* species and cultivars feature in every winter border. The brightly coloured stems light up the garden in winter. For large borders these always look the most impressive when planted in multiples of three, five, seven, etc. You need to add evergreens for balance, but they should not comprise more than one third of the total planting, or the border will look too 'heavy'. Ideal evergreens include *Cotoneaster* species with the added benefit of berries in the autumn, *Mahonia* species for their scented yellow flowers, which make attractive table decorations in winter combined with the soft pink flowers of *Viburnum bodnantense* and pure white snowdrops. *Lonicera fragrantissima* and *Sarcococca* species are also scented and winter flowering. The catkins of contorted *Corylus* cultivars look stunning in late winter after you have enjoyed the twisted stems. Hellebores should not be overlooked, as they flower over a long period and the flowers appear in a myriad of colours literally from white to black, single and double.

Cornus alba 'Westonbirt'. (Harveys Garden Plants)

7 PREPARING THE SITE

It is vital to prepare the new border carefully. A lot of time and money goes into establishing and maintaining a border, and if you do not start it off properly you may be setting up insoluble problems for later. The more effort you give to the preparation stage of the new border the more you will be rewarded in the growth and flowering of the plants, particularly in the first few years after planting.

REMOVE ALL WEEDS

You must take time to remove all of the perennial weeds before even thinking about planting. In particular, you may be considering saving plants from an overgrown border, to split and replant in the new border. Sometimes this is worthwhile and can save money. However beware of these weeds and especially take note of the procedure to eradicate them as described below.

One if these perennial weeds is ground elder (*Aegopodium podagraria*), a perennial plant in the carrot family (Apiaceae) that grows predominantly in shady places. Couch grass or twitch (*Elytrigia repens*) and creeping thistle (*Cirsium arvense*) are other invasive weeds that need to be removed before planting. The network of rhizomes becomes entangled in clumps of herbaceous perennials and among shrubs and fruit bushes, causing great problems as they are difficult to remove. Couch can easily spread from infested lawns into adjacent borders. It is usually spread from garden to garden unwittingly when small sections of rhizomes become hidden among the roots of plants, or in manures or soil. Couch is self-sterile and, as each spreading colony is usually a single clone, seeds are not often produced.

SEPARATING THE WEEDS FROM THE PLANTS

Couch grass and ground elder in particular are difficult to remove from established clumps. The following procedure is the only way to ensure the removal of these weeds from your plants:

- Dig up the desired clump; divide into two or three pieces; identify the invasive weed's root system and remove as much soil as possible by hand.
- Wash off the remainder, ensuring that all of the weed roots are removed.
- Replant in a nursery bed whilst the border preparations are carried out.
- Monitor the growth of the plant, and extract any weed shoots and roots which subsequently grow.

If this process is not carried out and the uncleaned clumps are replanted, in a short period of time the border will be a disaster, full of these invasive perennial weeds. Sometimes there is no alternative but to throw the clump away. (Do not be tempted to place it in your compost heap in the belief that all the roots will die if buried sufficiently; some of the roots will inevitably survive!)

OPPOSITE: **Sun loving plants. (Harpur Garden Images)**

Chemical Removal of Perennial Weeds

There are several effective ways to remove these perennial weeds, using safe chemical treatments.

Once you have removed any perennials you wish to keep, and you want to kill any remaining plants as well as the weeds, you can spray the entire border with the herbicide glyphosate (commonly sold as Round-up). This is a systemic herbicide, which means that when the product is sprayed onto the green leaf the material is translocated down into the roots and kills the plant. It has a low mammalian toxicity and is therefore relatively safe to humans and other mammals, and it has also a minimal effect on aquatic life too. Always follow manufacturer's label recommendations.

It is important to remember that this herbicide is only effective if the plant is actively growing – the weeds should have 10–15cm of shoot and leaf growth.

Rainfall affects success: During dry weather the percentage kill will be lower if the product is applied to plants that are droughted. Also after spraying ideally twenty-four hours should elapse before rain arrives, as rain will wash some of the herbicide from the leaf before it has been absorbed and thus render it less effective.

Seasonal variations: Glyphosate is most effective in early autumn when these plants are actively transporting sugars manufactured in the leaves down to the perennial root system – the storage of this 'food' in the root system enables the plant to over-winter with no foliage – so the glyphosate is also transported down to the furthest parts of the root system enabling a high percentage of kill. Conversely spraying in the spring is less effective as the plant is working hard to send nutrients and sugars stored in the root system up to the leaves, and thus the glyphosate is unlikely to reach the farthest part of the long roots underground. This will result in a lower percentage kill.

Remember even a high level of kill, say 98 per cent, will still leave some roots alive, and the plant will need respraying or removing by hand when the shoots reappear.

After an average time of three weeks has elapsed cultivations can start.

For new borders prepared from grass or rough ground, likewise it is advisable to spray the area with glyphosate about three weeks before work is intended to start. This gives the herbicide time to work and kill the weeds. If 100 per cent kill is not achieved, the remaining weeds can be killed with the subsequent cultivations.

Non-Chemical Removal of Perennial Weeds

If you prefer not to use chemicals there are alternatives.

You can cover the problem areas with old carpet. By excluding light this does not enable the weeds to grow, and slowly kills them. It can take up to six months for this method to be effective.

In uncultivated areas, forking out is possible in lighter soils. However forking out is much more difficult on heavy soils, as a lot of the underground stem system is fairly shallow and it is easy to leave behind small sections of rhizome which quickly regrow and need to be removed before they form a new network of rhizomes.

In cultivated areas, hand weeding can be done where there are small isolated infestations among herbaceous perennials. This is best done in early spring when the plants will soon re-establish, and around bulbs as the bulb foliage is dying, but is not practical around trees, shrubs and roses where roots may be considerably damaged.

If you are preparing borders from grass and you do not wish to use glyphosate then another alternative is to use a turf stripper. These are readily available from tool hire outlets on a daily basis, and at reasonable cost. This machine strips off the turf and roots, leaving soil below which can then be cultivated in the normal way. If the ground is compacted and dry, be aware that the turf stripper will be less efficient. The turf can be composted by making a mound laying each sod of turf upside down, and after a couple of years this highly fertile soil can be reused.

WHEN TO PREPARE BORDERS

The optimum timing for cultivating the new border depends on your soil type. For heavy clay based soils that have not been improved with compost or manure over the years, the timing is much more constricted than lighter sandy soils.

Heavy Clay Soils

The optimum time to prepare these difficult soils depends to some extent on the size of the border. For large borders (say over 10m in length and 3m wide) a mechanical digger would be advisable. To avoid undue mess in the garden it is advisable for the digger to carry out the preparations during the summer when the ground is hard, and the land is cracking open – during the summer my gardens show cracks of up to 5cm wide. Needless to say I garden on sticky heavy clay soil, which is great for growing plants in a drought, providing plenty of compost and manure has been added to the soil during the border preparations.

Cultivations should be carried out to a mini-mum depth of one fork, that is, 25cm. In summer the soil below this should be fissuring naturally and therefore there should not be any need to cultivate deeper unless you come across a 'pan' (a compacted layer of soil that shows anaerobic bacterial action, often caused by successive years of cultivating to the same depth). This can often be a problem when cultivating newly acquired farmland where the farmer has not used a piece of tillage machinery called a 'sub-soiler' to break up this compacted layer of soil. It will then be necessary to break it up using deeper cultiva-tions. If this is not carried out then plant roots will have difficulty in passing this hard, and typi-cally anaerobic, layer of soil. Typically the digger will produce large, hard clods, sometimes up to 25cm diameter. These are impossible to break up until weathering has taken place during the winter. So if a mechanical digger is used to prepare the borders, be prepared to wait until spring to plant.

In the spring, once the land has dried, a couple of passes with a rotovator as recommended below will typically have the borders ready for planting.

Heavy soil after manuring and having been turned over with a heavy mechanical digger. (Harveys Garden Plants)

DIGGER MAKES LIGHT WORK

If you are planning extensive borders then it is probably advisable to use large machinery, such as a digger, especially if the soil has not been cultivated for some considerable time. This is much easier than hand digging, and you can cultivate to the required depth and mix in compost and manure at the same time.

After this work the border will inevitably consist of large clods and clumps of manure. It should then be left to 'weather' – this is a process whereby the soil will break down into smaller clods by continual wetting and drying and fracturing by frost action if left during the winter. After a few months the soil and manure can be cultivated using a smaller garden rotovator.

Large mechanical digger. (Harveys Garden Plants)

For smaller borders or for those that have been tilled before, where the soil is not difficult to manipulate, the ideal method is a powerful garden rotovator (with a horse-power rating of about 5hp). These are also readily available from tool hire outlets. It needs to be of sufficient power to cultivate the soil properly. Again the soil needs to be cultivated to a depth of 25 cm if possible. The time of year when it is possible to use a rotovator is much wider than for a large digger.

Once the soils have dried sufficiently in the spring, then you can cultivate to produce a planting medium. Heavy soils can stay wet for a long time and it may not be possible to cultivate until late April or even May if the spring is particularly wet. To help speed up the drying of the soil in the spring you may choose in late winter to lift some of the soil by hand, that is, turn over the soil to reveal large clods and make the surface uneven so drying winds can penetrate the soil and dry it much quicker. If large clods are revealed, then weathering by frost and repeated drying and wetting by rain will help to break down the soil naturally.

In mid summer the soil will probably be too hard to rotovate, so the next opportunity will be early autumn, after the first rains have softened the soil. Remember though that after about 50mm of rain the soil will become too wet to cultivate and thus planting will be delayed until the spring. This happens typically in East Anglia by the end of October. After a few passes with a rotovator the border should be ready for planting.

If digging by hand, good luck and try not to bend your spade or buckle a prong on your fork!

Light Sandy Soils

Sandy soils are much easier to prepare for planting, as usually large impenetrable clods are not produced unless you delve down into the subsoil. So weathering of the soil is generally not as necessary. In fact for these soils the only time when it is difficult to cultivate is during a prolonged dry spell in the summer, when indeed the soil may have dried 'rock hard'. Therefore in this case you may need to employ a mechanical digger to prepare the borders. Large clods will be produced but these will take a relatively short time to break apart. This process of 'weathering' can of course be speeded up with occasional watering if the weather remains dry. Sandy soils and especially fine sandy soils (silts) are more prone to compaction, so it is important to ensure that good drainage is provided by breaking the soil pan if present. If digging by hand, it is essential that a fork penetrates this layer after turning over the top soil. This should be sufficient to 'Bust the Pan'.

Creating an Acidic Soil Pocket

Whilst I am not an advocate of growing acid loving plants in alkaline soil, it is possible to grow these plants if you create the right soil conditions. Usually, the best collections of acid loving plants are found in the wetter parts of the country, as many of these plants are evergreen and have leath-

ery leaves and therefore grow at their best with regular rainfall. Contrast East Anglia, with an annual rainfall of around 50mm per year, with Cornwall with an annual rainfall of over 100mm per year.

For example, to grow azaleas and rhododendrons successfully in a non-indigenous soil this is what you need to do:

1. Remove sufficient soil so the desired plants can reach a mature size; that is, for an azalea growing to about 1200mm remove up to 1 cubic metre of soil, typically to a depth of 800mm. This will enable some ground cover plants to be added, to complete the picture.
2. Back-fill with ericaceous compost or peat with a pH of about 5. (Bags of ericaceous compost are readily available from garden centres.) If the material to be back-filled has a pH of 6 or above, there is a risk that over time the pH will increase to over 7 (neutral) and will render alkaline your carefully crafted pocket of soil – and therefore your acid loving plants will die.
3. Watering: Typically, mains water and borehole supplies from areas of the country where the soils are generally alkaline will inevitably be alkaline too. If this water is used to irrigate your acid loving plants then over a period of time the compost will become alkaline. To avoid this you should water these plants with soft water, that is, rainwater from an underground storage tank or from a water butt.

An alternative, and simpler, way to grow these plants is in pots and containers filled with ericaceous soil. Soft water from a water butt should especially be used to water these pots.

Border Edges

It is important to create a distinct edge to the border so that you can stop weeds and grass encroaching into its soil. Creeping buttercup and couch grass are particular problems, especially if they are growing in your mown grass.

The edge can be created quite simply by cutting

Magnolia trasnokoensis.
(Harveys Garden Plants)

a V shape to the edge of the grass, using an edging spade. After mowing you can then cut the edge of the grass with edging shears, to keep the V shape free from interference.

If you prefer, there is also a range of products to keep the edge distinct. Probably one of the best systems is called 'Ever Edge' whereby a series of metal edges are linked together and then slotted into the edge of the grass. This has the benefit of preventing the grass edge from failing by collapse, and the grass can be trimmed easily. On the downside, it is relatively expensive. Another method sometimes adopted is to use treated wood and stakes. It is possible to use treated timber – around 15mm thick, 100mm deep and of any required length – to form the edge, which is then periodically staked with narrow posts. If you have

to negotiate round edged borders, you can create bendable edging by repeatedly partially sawing the timber through on one side to form lots of small cuts; the timber will then readily bend to fit the curvature.

If you are planning an underground irrigation system, it should be constructed during these border preparations; *see* Chapter 2 for further consideration of some of the options available.

MANURES, COMPOSTS AND SOIL IMPROVERS

It is essential to include soil improvement in border preparations. Plants will establish better, grow quicker, and thus inhibit weed growth, resulting in less time weeding during the first few years. However, bear in mind that manures, composts and soil improvers do not usually contain large amounts of plant nutrients, with the exception of poultry manure which is rich in nitrogen. It is not balanced, since it contains low levels of potash, phosphate and trace elements which are essential for plant growth. So composts and manures should be thought of as soil conditioners rather than supplies of nutrients. For heavy clay soils they help to improve the soil structure by opening up the soil and letting more air to circulate. This enables one to work on the soil for longer than otherwise expected. For light sandy soils the addition of composts improves the water retentive qualities, and thus improves the growth of plants and subsequent flowering. It may even improve the range of summer flowering plants one can grow successfully on these soils that are so prone to drought.

Manure

Manure produced by animals is particularly useful, provided it is well rotted. This may take up to twelve months before the manure is useable – eighteen months is better. My rule of thumb is that if the manure still smells when you are applying it, then it is probably not well rotten. The best manure is produced by bullocks, when overwintered in straw cattle yards. Of similar quality is horse manure if the horses are stabled using straw. If woodchip is used as bedding then avoid using it as manure, because the bacteria and fungi decomposing the woodchip will take nutrients out of the soil, thus depleting the available nutrients plants need to grow; this can result in plants becoming chlorosed and yellow, resulting in poor flowering and a lack of seeds. Pig manure is not ideal, as the resultant product is too wet.

Poultry and turkey manure are high in ammonical nitrogen. Therefore even after composting it needs to be used sparingly, as this form of nitrogen is unavailable to plants, and burns roots. When adequately composted, the ammonical nitrogen is broken down to a usable form by soil microbes; however if used liberally then excessive and soft growth will occur that will cause plants to fall over.

In recent years there has been concern over grass sprayed with certain agricultural herbicides. The degradation products have caused probems for gardeners when cattle have been fed with this grass, either as hay or silage. In 2008, allotment holders and gardeners reported that their crops were showing unusual symptoms; the cause turned out to be manure contaminated with the very persistent weedkiller aminopyralid. Dow Agrosciences introduced stringent conditions regarding the use of aminopyralid, to prevent it getting into manures, but there have been subsequent reports of further damage. The Soil Association and Organic Growers Alliance (OGA) has called upon gardeners and growers to be on the lookout for symptoms on susceptible crops, including twisted, cupped, and elongated leaves; misshapen fruit; reduced yield; death of young plants; and poor seed germination. Concern also exists over the residues from herbicides containing chlorpyralid.

Composts

If you have sufficient room in your own garden, then the best and safest forms of soil conditioner will be derived from making your own. Small tumbling compost makers can be purchased which turn kitchen green waste into compost in a matter of weeks. Alternatively build your own compost bins, either from preservative treated slatted timber (do not use creosote or other similar product which is harmful to plants) or modified pallets. For large gardens make a series of boxes from pallets covered in wire-netting on the outside to provide an economical way of making your own compost bins.

Other ingenious designs are available, such as a Bee-hive – you can add sections to make the compost bin taller, just the same as you could with a normal wooden bee-hive.

Regular turning of the compost with the addition of some fertilizer (inorganic Growmore, or equivalent) readily speeds up the transformation of additions such as grass clippings into

Large compost bins. (Harveys Garden Plants)

useful compost. A handful of small blood worms dramatically increases the rate of breakdown too. Ideally three boxes should be provided: one contains composted material, ready to use; the second is filled and composting; and the third is in the process of being filled. A cover is beneficial to limit the amount of rain penetrating the compost so that it does not become too soggy; old carpet is often used for this purpose.

Spent mushroom compost is often available from adverts in your local paper. This is a useful material, providing it has been composted for at least six months. However, if the compost comes straight from the mushroom factory, it is high in ammonical nitrogen, and if applied to the soil into which plants are to be planted soon after, problems will occur. The plants will fail to root properly, as this form of nitrogen will burn the roots and may cause the plants to die rapidly. Watering the plants thoroughly will not overcome the problem.

Soil Improvers

'Soil improver' is a term usually applied to the

Bee-hive compost bin. (Harveys Garden Plants)

Bee-hive compost bin in use. (Harveys Garden Plants)

conversion of domestic green waste into a useful product and often sold at council refuse sites. It can be variable, but is an ideal alternative to animal manure (especially if you do not know the provenance of the material, as described previously) or to making your own compost. It is usually available in conveniently sized 25L bags, which are easy to handle and economically priced. You can also buy this material in bulk, which saves having to open loads of bags and avoids generating plastic waste. When buying in bulk it is as well to ask about the quality. I have had a couple of experiences when the delivery to a client included all manor of rubbish including parts of mobile phones, mustard spoons (not silver unfortunately), lots of shreds of plastic and much more. Not ideal. However it is a product I am sure we shall all use more extensively in the future.

Compost or manures should be applied after the initial soil preparations, and before planting. Copious amounts of organic material applied will result in amazing growth even in the first year. A minimum of 10cm (preferably 15cm) laid on top of the whole bed is ideal. Then either fork or rotovate this into the soil, and the preparations are complete.

BUYING PLANTS

Now we are approaching the fun element for most gardeners. Once you have decided on the plants and the numbers required it is time to order these from your chosen specialist nurseries or visit your local garden centre to select your favourite plants. It is easier to work with a few selected and trusted nurseries rather than selecting plants from encyclopaedias and then trying to find them, as many of these plants are difficult to source.

At the beginning of the planting season in spring and autumn there is a greater variety of shrubs and perennials generally available, so if possible order well in advance of your anticipated planting date.

If you are buying plants off the shelf, look for good sized specimens that are full in their pots and yet not pot-bound. Another consideration is to choose plants that have more than just one flower stem with no basal growth. Plants that have bolted to make a quick flower are unlikely to survive the first winter. Many of the new exotic coloured cultivars of echinacea have this attribute. The survival rates can be improved by cutting down the flower stem by half. This will encourage basal growth, and new flowers will appear in due course form the leaf petioles on the remaining stem.

Although most gardeners would like an instant border in year one, full of colour and interesting shapes, in practice this can only be achieved by purchasing large plants. If these are planted in the autumn, then these prized specimens will have the winter to begin rooting into the soil and more likely to survive a drought the following year. This

Buying of plants from a specialist nursery. (Harveys Garden Plants)

Echinacea 'Tomato Soup'. (Cotswold Garden Flowers)

Echinacea purpurea 'Coconut Lime'. (Cotswold Garden Flowers)

is particularly important for large shrubs. However if you establish the borders in late spring without an irrigation system, then large plants will need more attention especially during the first year, as they will not have a sufficiently developed root system compared to the foliage generated.

The only exceptions to this are some perennials that, although perfectly hardy once established, may be lost if planted late in the autumn. For example agapanthus hybrids are generally hardy, except *Agapanthus africanus* which is not; this plant is characterized by having large wide leaves of up to 30mm across and large blue flowers in late summer. Apart from the West Country this plant should be grown in large pots which in late autumn can then be transferred to a greenhouse which should be kept frost-free.

Echinacea 'Razzamatazz'. (Cotswold Garden Flowers)

8 PLANTING YOUR BORDERS

WHEN IS THE BEST TIME TO PLANT?

This is an age-old conundrum. Many observers and 'gardening experts' advise planting in the spring. However I am not an advocate of this catch-all suggestion. There are lots of variables to take into account, and many of these revolve around your own life-style.

One of the first points to consider is the make-up of the border. If you have a large border with lots of shrubs to plant, then the optimum time to plant these is in early autumn, probably October. This gives these large plants time to settle in and start to root over the winter. They will then require less attention than shrubs planted in the spring which will require regular watering. However if you decide to create a new border at other times of the year and you are prepared to provide regular watering, whether it be in the form of irrigation or watering by hand, then as nearly all shrubs are pot grown, you can theoretically plant at any time of the year.

Also of equal importance is the quality of your soil. Whilst the time of year for planting is a factor, perhaps of more relevance is the suitability of the soil for planting – in particular, is it too dry or is it too wet? With climate change now firmly acknowledged, it is becoming apparent that we are faced with more extremes of weather. For example on occasion the climate in East Anglia has varied from dry springs and wet summers to wet springs and dry summers. This makes forecasting when to plant unpredictable.

OPPOSITE: *Hemerocallis* cultivars spilling over the brick path creating a soft edge.

Do not water the borders before planting as this makes the soil wet. When you then tread onto the soil to plant, you compact the wonderful structure that may have taken you weeks to prepare. As a consequence plants do not give of their best.

If you plan to go on holiday it is advisable not plant extensively, especially if you are taking a long break. Neighbours are unlikely to water the garden as effectively as the owners, and irrigation systems are not fool-proof; they do go wrong and therefore need checking periodically.

You may consider planting for a special event. This is certainly a popular option on occasion. The important consideration, as discussed above, is the quality of the soil at the time of planting. If you require the border to be in full flower at any given time, plants will need to be selected carefully to achieve this.

HOW TO PLANT

Ideal Tools

Comfortable gardening tools are essential to give the gardener pleasure no matter what the job. For planting I tend to use a 'Ladies' spade and fork' and a narrow pointed trowel; these are ideal since most of the plants to be planted will be in pots not larger than 2/3 litre. Stainless tools tend to be easier to use on heavy soils, as the sticky soil will glide past the implement and not stick to it.

Older tools that have been reclaimed from a bygone age are a treat to use, as the wooden handles have been worn smooth with years of service. These tools appear at specialist auctions, and antique dealers from all over the country. The quality of the forged steel certainly surpasses most

GIVE THEM A GOOD DRINK

Once you have got your plants home, water them thoroughly. Some pots of plants may be extremely dry, and watering from above will not be sufficient. Place the plant/s in a bucket or tray of water so that half of the pot is submerged. Then water the top of the plant, so the soil is wetted through. The water applied to the top of the plant is unlikely to have penetrated more than 2.5cm, thus most of the plant will still be dry. The water in the bucket will be taken up by the compost as far as the water-line in the bucket, and because you wetted the top of the plant water will be drawn up by capillary action to this wetted layer in the pot, ensuring thorough wetting of the compost. If this is not carried out then the dry plants may not get sufficient wetting when planted into the soil.

tools made today – I have yet to come across forks with bent tines or spades whereby the steel has bent inexplicably. The handles are comfortable and will continue to give years of great service. Finally when you have finished with them (if ever) they can be passed onto keen family members and treasured as heirlooms.

SEEING RED

To avoid losing tools in the garden, it is advisable never to place secateurs, hand tools and other favourite items in the wheelbarrow with the weeds or especially with the cuttings destined for the bonfire. At our nursery, missing tools can often be found in the fire ash, minus their wooden handles! The choice of brightly coloured handles for these tools helps considerably; for instance the handles of Felco secateurs are coloured red.

The only secateurs I would recommend are those made by the Swiss company Felco. They offer a range of sizes, shapes and even left-handed secateurs, and their tools go on for ever. Should they need repairs then the company currently offers a free service. They also offer sharpening tools, which are well worth the cost for a lifetime's service.

Plants placed close to the border. (Harpur Garden Images)

Placing the Plants

Place the plants near the border, so they are close to hand.

Arrange the plan in a convenient position in front of the border (with the corners weighted to avoid the plan being blown away).

Take the plants that you have planned to give structure (this may be the largest shrubs or the largest perennials) and position them according to the plan. If these plants are not immediately available then you can use canes to identify the correct planting position temporarily so the rest

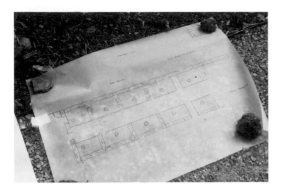

The border plan. (Harpur Garden Images)

Starting to lay out plants. (Harpur Garden Images)

of the planting may continue. Short canes up to 25cm long are ideal – if you use longer canes then be careful when bending down near these canes so as not to cause injury to eyes and other parts of the face. Ornamental or plain cane toppers can now be purchased and placed over the top of the cane to avoid such injuries.

It is sometimes helpful to then move to the front of the border and start placing plants so the correct spacing can be achieved. This will ensure the plants at the front of the border do not over-hang onto the grass or pathway unless intended. A good idea to achieve exact spacing of plants in a formal setting is to cut a piece of cane to the desired length and insert this between plants as you place the plants in position

Short canes ae ideal for marking the position of plants. (Harpur Garden Images)

Correct spacing of plants at the front of the border. (Harpur Garden Images)

Starting to lay out plants. (Harpur Garden Images)

Having planted some plants at the front of the border, you can then start positioning plants in between the plants at the front and the taller plants in the middle or rear of the border, remembering to plant perennials in drifts and not just in the classic triangles. It helps to consider the border as a piece of art and the drifts of plants likened to brush strokes.

Only after all of the plants have been positioned, and you are happy with considerations such as the sequence of flowering and contrasting shapes, should the planting be started. Remember the plan does not have to be adhered to at any cost. Think of it as more of a starting point. There will inevitably be situations whereby you discover that the choice of plant neighbours is not quite right. You may find that inadvertently two variegated plant cultivars have been placed next to one another, or there are colour clashes which you had not predicted. This happens. So the main criteria is to remain flexible and adjust your planting as necessary.

Planting

Planting depth is important. For most plants the hole to be dug should be large enough for the plant to fit in comfortably, and when planted there should be a covering of about 15mm of soil over the top of the surface of the plant. Later as the soil settles, the top of the plant does not want to be visible above the soil, as this will lead to increased evaporation of water and an unsightly planting of the border.

Use fertilizer for shrubs but not perennials. Apply a trowel of slow-release fertilizer such as bonemeal to the soil that has been dug out of the hole to allow the shrub to be planted. Then backfill around the shrub with this nutritious soil. The shrub roots will find the dispersed fertilizer and grow vigorously. As discussed earlier, it is not generally recommended that fertilizer is applied to perennial plantings as this will lead to excessive soft growth and many plants failing to stay upright.

Watering is essential. After all of the plants have been planted you should 'water in' each plant to make sure there are no excessive air gaps around the roots. Failure to do this can lead to excessive drying out of the root ball, and may result in the death of the plant. Even if rain is forecast it is still recommended to water in your new plantings. Then depending on the time of year when you are planting and the size of plants, you can assess the amount of subsequent watering required.

Moles can pose a particular problem after

planting. They mine the soil looking for worms, and they like the loose soil that you have prepared. As a consequence the mole tracks introduce exces-sie air into the soil, which dries the roots and can easily lead to the death of many plants. To avoid this, monitor mole hills and check that the soil remains firm around the new plantings; this may need to be checked frequently over the first few years. Ideally humanely catch the troublesome moles and dispose of appropriately. Remember moles can travel over three miles looking for suit-able 'homes'

MULCHING AFTER PLANTING

Sometimes mulching is appropriate, and if it is a good idea for your border there are various types of mulch available, from bark to different coloured stones, gravels and slate. A selection will be covered here.

Mulches should be applied in late spring as the plants emerge from winter, which will enable you to avoid covering the emerging perennials. The other benefit of applying the mulch in late spring is that it locks in the soil moisture which should be high after the winter rains. The depth of mulch is important. Too little and you do not suppress the weeds; too much and the plants become buried.

Bark Mulches

The ideal type of bark mulch is 'composted bark', which has been shredded and chipped to make small pieces, and together with some bark 'fines' (slightly larger than sawdust) composted for at least one year. It is almost black in colour and

THE PROBLEM WITH WOODCHIP

Bark mulch should not contain woodchip, which is a real problem for gardeners if used as a mulch. This is because the bacte-ria and fungi extract nitrogen and other essential nutrients from the soil to break down the cellulose in the white heartwood chips of the felled tree (woodchip). This process takes many years to complete as cellulose is one of natures slowest materi-als to degrade. Good composted bark on the other hand contains little or no wood-chip, and the bacteria and fungi do not need to extract nutrients from the soil as they are available in this medium.

While woodchip should not be used as mulch, it does make a good material for natural looking paths, particularly in wood-land, where the rainfall is limited. However if you expect heavy foot-traffic (footfall) then this material will quickly sink into the ground and therefore the path will become soggy and unusable during rainy periods.

Summer flowering perennials. (Harpur Garden Images)

contains lots of fungi and bacteria breaking down the bark material.

Bark mulches should be laid at no more than 30mm deep. If you have used a seep hose irrigation system and laid the pipes on top of the soil, then a composted bark mulch may be ideal to hide these ugly black pipes. Blackbirds in particular enjoy pulling the bark about looking for insects underneath. This means that bark can be scattered all over the garden – not desirable if you are a tidy gardener.

Wood chip composting. (Harveys Garden Plants)

Gravel

There are several different sizes, colours and types of gravel available. As a general rule local stone fits into the natural landscape better than something that has to be brought from across the country. For example in East Anglia the natural stone is flint. Therefore the stone products that are extracted from the local gravel pits are a series of flint gravels. After washing, this gravel fits into the garden landscape quite naturally as flint pebbles and boulders may already be present in the garden. Contrast this with blue slate slithers that have been shipped from Wales and further away. Environmentally this does not make sense and this mulch looks quite artificial in the East Anglian landscape.

Gravel is often applied to a border to give a more Mediterranean feel. The planting therefore has to be chosen appropriately and ideally to have a flavour of the Mediterranean. For example if the border is in a sunny position then perennial herbs

are ideal, such as *Salvia* species (sage), *Lavendula* cultivars (lavender), *Thymus* cultivars (thyme) and *Rosmarinus* cultivars (rosemary). Other plants such as Eryngiums and some of the smaller grasses *Helictotrichon sempervirens* and *Stipa tenuissima* are ideal.

Gravel mulched border lightly planted. (Harveys Garden Plants)

Creating a Gravel Border

Creating a gravel border successfully is more difficult than just applying a bark mulch to an existing border. To avoid worm action spoiling the finished

Pegged membrane. (Harveys Garden Plants)

Plants placed on membrane. (Harveys Garden Plants)

again fold down the cut edge to reduce frayed edges being exposed. At the same time you need to minimize the area of bare soil exposed at the base of the plant, to reduce weed growth.

Finished planting. (Harveys Garden Plants)

look, with worm casts appearing on top of the gravel, you should do the following:

First, place a porous membrane over the entire border and peg this down with special clips; remember to fold under any cut edges as these will fray and cause a nuisance.

Place the plants on top of the membrane, at the correct spacing. Space plants within a group at the normal spacing, but leave areas unplanted to expose the gravel once it has been applied; this leads to a more open style of border.

Underneath each plant cut a cross with a pair of scissors and peel back the membrane; this gives access to the soil below.

Then plant the plants in the usual fashion, and pull the membrane back to the base of the plant;

Planting through the membrane. (Harveys Garden Plants)

Finished border. (Harveys Garden Plants)

Water trickling over a millstone. (Design: Annabel Fife, Yorks)

After all the plants have been planted apply the gravel mulch to a depth of about 25mm.

The plants can grow and form a good clump, deriving rain as it passes through the porous membrane.

Sometimes gatherings of beach cobbles presented in a naturalistic fashion just finish off the border to great effect. For an exotic finish, coloured gravels and slate can be used. The colour of these needs to be carefully considered in relation to where the border is positioned within the garden and in relation to the chosen plants in the border. Often a gravel border within the garden will be near hard landscaping or near the house. It would be a mistake to locate it in the middle of a country garden, as it would look completely out of place and unnatural.

A simple water feature as part of this design can look stunning. Water trickling over a large rock or millstone can add a sense of tranquillity.

MAINTENANCE OF THE NEW BORDER

Maintaining the new border's fabulous ambiance is important and need not be arduous, as you have carefully selected the right plant for the right place.

If you are not familiar with the fine details of the plants you have used, then it is worth while making another list of the plants used in the borders, and then detailing alongside each entry the suggested pruning times, and maybe further cultural notes, for example with reference to when these plants may be propagated or divided to maintain vigour. You could also include possible pests that may attack each species of plant. With this information you can keep your plants healthy and vigorous with a minimum of concern.

Sometimes unwelcome visitors such as muntjac deer will appear in the garden. Muntjac, also known as barking deer, are voracious and will eat a large range of shrubs, perennials and vegetables. They can jump 2m fences and so are hard to keep out of the garden. However deer and in particular muntjac do not like 'scented' soap. Try this method, using inexpensive supermarket soap: cut each bar in half with a saw; drill a hole in the middle of each half bar of sufficient size to take a piece of wire; thread a length of wire through each bar of soap and tie it to small posts or trees at intervals of about 2m around the area you wish to protect, at a height of about 70cm from the ground. This can also be applied to individual trees, for example if you are planting a new orchard. Rabbits, deer and hares are more of a problem. Even if the whole garden is netted they still find their way in, so if these animals are prevalent a small wire netting enclosure to a height of 60cm around the new border/s may be the only option for the first couple of years. After this period these pests tend not to be so interested, and therefore the netting can be removed.

A well planned border or series of borders and executed with love and care will provide the owner with years of pride and enjoyment. Environmental friends such as bees, butterflies and other small mammals will visit and enhance your

A newly planted garden. (Harveys Garden Plants)

satisfaction, knowing you have created something worthwhile for them too. Friends will marvel at your newfound ability, and it will not be long before you will be seconded to help create similar extravaganzas in their gardens.

A mature border of perennials and grasses after three years. (Harveys Garden Plants)

The gazebo border in high summer at Harveys Garden Plants. (Harveys Garden Plants)

APPENDIX: PLANTS SUITABLE FOR VARIOUS ASPECTS AND SOIL TYPES

The tables in this Appendix contain a wide range of plants with concise details, and are designed to help the reader to design their border or borders using easy to grow plants. This can be used as a short cut to my suggestion in Chapter 3 to construct lists of suitable plants and then to choose your favourites accordingly. All the key elements to designing a border that works are listed here, for example, the approximate size of the plant given good growing conditions, the time of flowering (to aid the design of year round interest) and the colour of the flower, including foliage. Further information on important aspects, such as soil pH and soil type, are presented in Chapter 2.

Herbaceous borders in late summer. (Harveys Garden Plants)

PERENNIALS
Shade Tolerant Perennials for Clay and Loam Soils

PLANT NAME	Height mm	Spread mm	Flower colour	Scent	Month of Flowering	Evergreen	Deciduous	Leaf Interest	
Anemone *nemerosa*	100	150	white		April		✓		Dies down in June / Native wood anemone
Anemone *nemerosa* 'Royal Blue'	100	150	mid blue		April		✓		Dies down in June
Anemone *ranunculoides*	100	150	yellow		April		✓		Dies down in June
Arisaema *sikokianum*	400	300	purple/white		May		✓		Plant on bed of grit
Arisarum *proboscideum*	100	100	white/brown		April		✓		Long brown 'mouse' tails / Dies down in summer
Arum *italicum* spp. *italicum* 'Marmoratum'	200	200	white		April		✓	leaves marbled with cream	Red berries in summer/autumn / Dies down in June
Aruncus *dioicus*	130	100	white		July		✓		Damp position / The goat's beard
Asarum *arifolium*	150	300	red		March	✓			Good ground cover
Asarum *splendens*	150	300	brown/white		March	✓		large kidneyshaped	Large brown flowers
Asplenium *scolopendrium*	300	300				✓			Native harts tongue fern
Brunnera 'Betty Bowring'	500	500	white		April		✓		
Brunnera 'Jack Frost'	500	500	blue		April		✓	silver leaves/ green edge	
Dryopteris *affinis* 'Cristata'	1000	1000				✓			Elegant

PLANT NAME	Height mm	Spread mm	Flower colour	Scent	Month of Flowering	Evergreen	Deciduous	Leaf Interest	COMMENTS
Dryopteris erythrosora	400	400				✓			Fern young fronds rosy-brown
Epimedium flavum OG 92.036	200	200	clear yellow		April	✓			
Epimedium fargesii	500	500	white/deep purple		April		✓		
Epimedium grandiflorum 'Lilafee'	400	400	purple		April		✓	purple flushed	
Epimedium perralchicum 'Frohnleiten'	200	600	yellow		April	✓			Stoloniferous
Geranium macrorrhizum album	500	500	off white		May	✓		scented leaf	
Geranium macrorrhizum 'Ingwersen's Variety'	500	500	pale pink		May	✓		scented leaf	Stoloniferous
Geranium phaeum Samobor	800	700	purple		June		✓	chocolate blotched	
Helleborus foetidus	500	500	green		Jan-April	✓			
Hepatica nobilis	100	100	blue		February	✓			
Heuchera 'Midnight Rose'	250	250	pink		June	✓		red speckled, black/red leaves	
Hosta plantaginea var. *japonica*	600	600	white	✓	Sept		✓		
Hosta seiboldiana 'Elegans'	700	700	lilac-mauve		July		✓		
Hosta undulata var. *univittata* (variegata)	400	400	lilac		July		✓	cream variegated twisted leaves	
Hosta 'Halcyon'	600	600	lilac/blue		July		✓	blue leaves	

Plant			Flower colour	✓	Month	✓	Notes
Iris japonica 'Variegata'	600	600	blue/yellow/white		May	✓	boldly variegated leaves
Lamium orvala	600	600	red		April	✓	Moist soil
Lamium 'White Nancy'	150	150	white		June	✓	silvered leaves
Lilium martagon	2000	150	purple spotted		June	✓	Turks cap lilly
Maianthemum racemosa	700	600	white	✓	April		Rich soil
Matteuccia struthiopteris	1000	800				✓	Shuttlecock fern; shuttlecock fronds
Pachysandra procumbens	200	300	white/pink anthers	✓			Flowers smell of spice
Polystichum setiferum 'Divisilobum Group Herrenhausen'	800	1000				✓	Dry shade
Scopolia carniolica 'Zwanenburg'	700	700	maroon		April	✓	Poisonous
Smyrnium perfoliatum	800	200	acid green/yellow		May	✓	Tri-annual
Speirantha convallarioides	200	300	white	✓	May	✓	
Symphytum ibericum	300	600	white	✓	April		Burnt orange flower buds; Stoloniferous
Trillium cuneatum	400	400	brown/purple		April	✓	Troat lilly; Most soil neural to acid soil
Trillium grandiflorum	250	300	white		April	✓	Trout lilly; Most soil neural to acid soil
Trillium sulcatum	300	300	red		April	✓	Trout lilly; Moist soil neural to acid soil
Tricyrtis formosana 'Dark Beauty'	700	500	dark purple spots on white		Sept-Oct	✓	Toad lily retentive soil, stoloniferous
Viola 'Governor Herrick'	200	200	large blue		April/May	✓	
Viola labradorica	150	200	light purple		April	✓	
Viola odorata sulphurea	100	150	amber	✓	April		Good ground cover between shrubs

PERENNIALS
Shade Tolerant Perennials for Sandy Soils

PLANT NAME	Height mm	Spread mm	Flower colour	Scent	Month of Flowering	Evergreen	Deciduous	Leaf Interest	COMMENTS
Anemone nemerosa	100	150	white		April		✓		Dies down in June / Native wood anemone
Anemone nemerosa 'Virescens'	100	150	green		April		✓		Dies down in June
Anemone ranunculoides	100	150	yellow		April		✓		Dies down in June
Arisaema sikokianum	400	300	purple/white		May		✓		One of the best
Arisarum proboscideum	100	100	white/brown		April		✓		Long brown 'mouse' tails / Dies down in summer
Arum italicum spp. italicum 'Marmoratum'	200	200	white		April		✓	leaves marbled with cream	Red berries in summer/autumn / Dies down in June
Asplenium scolopendrium	300	300				✓			Native hearts tongue fern
Brunnera 'Betty Bowring'	500	500	white		April		✓		
Brunnera 'Jack Frost'	500	500	blue		April		✓	silver leaves/ green edge	
Convallaria majalis	150	150	white	✓	April	✓			Lilly of the valley
Convallaria majalis 'Albostriata'	150	150	white	✓	April	✓			
Dryopteris affinis 'Cristata'	1000	1000				✓			Elegant
Epimedium grandiflorum 'Lilafee'	400	400	purple		April		✓	purple flushed	
Epimedium perralchicum 'Frohnleiten'	200	600	yellow		April		✓		Stoloniferous

Plant			Colour	Month		Notes	Type
Epimedium versicolor 'Neosulphureum'	400	600	lemon yellow	April	✓		Stoloniferous
Euphorbia amygdaloides 'Robbiae'	600	1000	yellow/green	June	✓		Stoloniferous
Geranium macrorrhizum 'Ingwersen's variety'	500	500	pale pink	May	✓	scented leaf	Stoloniferous
Geranium phaeum 'Samobor'	800	700	purple	June	✓	chocolate blotched	
Helleborus foetidus	500	500	green	Jan-April	✓		
Heuchera 'Obsidian'	300	300	white	June	✓		
Hosta plantaginea var. *japonica*	600	600	white	Sept	•		
Hosta seiboldiana 'Elegans'	700	700	lilac-mauve	July	✓		
Hosta undulate var. *univittata* (variegate)	500	500	lilac	June	•	cream variegated leaves	
Hosta 'Halcyon'	600	600	lilac/blue	July	✓	blue leaves	
Lamium 'White Nancy'	150	150	white	June	✓	silvered leaves	
Lilium martagon	2000	150	purple spotted	June	✓	Turks cap lilly	
Pachyphragma macrophyllum	200	200	white	March	✓		
Pachysandra procumbens	200	300	white/pink anthers	✓	✓	Flowers smell of spice	
Polystichum setiferum 'Proliferum Group'	800	700			✓	Dry shade	
Smyrnium perfoliatum	800	200	acid green/yellow	May	✓	tri-annual	
Speirantha convallarioides	200	300	white	May	✓		
Symphytum ibericum	300	600	white	April	✓	Burnt orange flower buds	Stoloniferous
Viola 'Governor Herrick'	200	200	large blue	April/May	✓		
Viola odorata 'Perle Rose'	100	150	pink	April	✓		
Viola odorata sulphurea	100	150	amber	April	✓		

PERENNIALS
Semi-shade Tolerant Perennials for Clay/Loam Soils

PLANT NAME	Height mm	Spread mm	Flower colour	Scent	Month of Flowering	Evergreen	Deciduous	Leaf Interest	COMMENTS
Acanthus spinosus	1000	1000	mauve/white		July/Aug		✓	glossy, deep cut	Flowering better in full sun
Aconitum autumnale 'Bressingham Spire'	1200	700	blue		July/Aug		✓		Poisonous
Aconitum carmichaelii 'Arendsii'	1500	800	dark blue		Sept/Oct		✓		Poisonous
Allium christophii	500	200	lilac		June		✓		
Allium hollandicum 'Purple Sensation'	600	200	lilac/purple		May		✓		
Amsonia tabernaemontana	500	500	lilac		June		✓		
Anemone hupehensis 'September Charm'	800	800	single pink		Aug-Oct		✓		Stoloniferous good ground cover
Anemone leveillei	600	400	white/ blue reverse		May		✓		Clump forming
Anemone sylvestris	400	400	white satin		May		✓		Stoloniferous, good ground cover
Anemone × hybrida 'Pamina'	700	700	double pink		Aug-Oct		✓		Stoloniferous good ground cover
Anemone × hybrida 'Whirlwind'	800	800	semi-double white		Aug-Oct		✓		Stoloniferous good ground cover
Arisarum proboscideum	100	100	white/brown		April		✓		Long brown 'mouse' tails Dies down in summer
Arum italicum spp. italicum 'Marmoratum'	200	200	white		April		✓	leaves marbled with cream	Red berries in summer/autumn Dies down in June

Plant			Colour	Month		✓	Feature	Notes
Aruncus dioicus	1300	1000	white	July		✓		Damp position; The goat's beard
Asarum arifolium	150	300	red	March	✓			Good ground cover
Asarum splendens	150	300	brown/white	March	✓		large kidney shaped	Large brown flowers
Asplenum scolopendrium	300	300			✓			Native hearts tongue fern
Astrantia major 'Little Snowstar'	400	400	white	May/July		✓		
Astrantia major rosea	400	400	pink	May/July		✓		
Beesia calthifolia	400	400	starry white	May–Oct	✓		bronze marbled	Humous rich soil
Bergenia 'Overture'	300	300	deep magenta	Mar/April	✓		red foliage in winter	
Brunnera 'Betty Bowring'	500	500	white	April		✓		
Brunnera 'Jack Frost'	500	500	blue	April		✓	silver leaves/ green edge	
Campanula punctata 'Rubrifolia'	600	400	pink	June/July		✓		Stoloniferous red stems
Cyclamen coum	100	100	cerise-white	Feb/March		✓		
Cyclamen hederifolium	100	100	pink-white	Aug–Oct		✓	silvered/marbled	
Dicentra formosa	400	400	pink	April/May		✓		Good ground cover between shrubs
Dicentra spectablis	700	600	pink	April/May		✓		Rich soil
Dicentra spectablis 'Alba'	700	600	alba	April/May		✓		Rich soil
Digitalis mertonensis	800	500	dusky rose	June/July		✓		Biennial
Digitalis purpurea albiflora	1000	500	white	May		✓		Biennial
Disporopsis pernyi	400	300	white	June	✓	✓		
Disporum flavens	700	400	yellow	April		✓		
Disporum megalanthum	600	400	white	April		✓	dark foliage	
Epimedium grandiflorum 'Lilafee'	400	400	purple	April		✓	purple flushed	

PLANT NAME	Height mm	Spread mm	Flower colour	Scent	Month of Flowering	Evergreen	Deciduous	Leaf Interest	COMMENTS
Epimedium perralchicum 'Frohnleiten'	200	600	yellow		April	✓		red tinted foliage	Stoloniferous dry shade
Epimedium perralchicum 'Wisley'	200	600	yellow		April	✓		glossy green foliage	Stoloniferous dry shade
Epimedium versicolor 'Sulphureum'	400	600	yellow		April	✓			Stoloniferous dry shade
Erythronium californicum 'Harvington Snowgoose'	400	200	white		late April		✓	maroon markings	Elegant
Erythronium dens-canis 'Old Aberdeen'	150	200	vivid purple/rose		March		✓	chocolate marked	Dog tooth violet
Euphorbia amygdaloides 'Purpurea'	400	200	acid yellow/green		April	✓			
Euphorbia griffithii 'Dixter'	600	600	chestnut-tan		June		✓		
Fragaria vesca 'Variegata'	150	500	white		May		✓	striking variegated	Stoloniferous good ground cover between shrubs Alpine strawberries edible
Galanthus elwesii	150	200	white		Jan-April		✓		
Galanthus nivalis	100	200	white		Jan-April		✓		
Geranium cantabrigiense 'Cambridge'	300	500	mauve		May		✓	scented	
Geranium himalayense 'Gravetye'	300	300	blue				✓		
Geranium macrorrhizum 'Ingwersen's Variety'	500	500	pale pink		May	✓		scented leaf	Stoloniferous
Geranium macrorrhizum album	500	500	off white		May	✓		scented leaf	

Plant			Flower colour	Flowering			Foliage	Notes
Geranium 'Patrica'	600	700	magenta pink/indigo eye	June/July		✓		More compact than G. psilostemon
Geranium phaeum 'Samobor'	800	700	purple	June		✓	chocolate blotched	
Geranium psilostemon	700	800	magenta pink	June/July		✓		Rambling
Geum 'Leonard's Variety'	300	200	red	April		✓		
Geum 'Lionel Cox'	200	200	apricot	April		✓		
Gillenia trifoliata	700	700	white blush pink	June		✓		
Helleborus hybridus	400	600	white-black	Jan-April	✓			Flower colour in all shades
Helleborus 'Winter Moonbeam'	400	400	pink buds cream flowers	Feb/Apr	✓		marbled foliage	Flower colour matures to deep red
Helleborus 'Winter Sunshine'	400	400	pink buds cream flowers		✓		dark green foliage	Flower colour matures to deep red
Hepatica nobilis	100	100	blue	February	✓			
Heuchera 'Obsidian'	300	300	white	June	✓			
Hosta plantaginea var. japonica	600	600	white	Sept	✓	✓		Will tolerate sun
Hosta seiboldiana 'Elegans'	700	700	lilac/mauve	July		✓		
Hosta undulata var. univittata (variegata)	500	500	lilac	July		✓	Cream variegated twisted leaves	
Hosta 'Halcyon'	600	600	lilac/blue	July		✓	blue leaves	
Lamium 'White Nancy'	150	150	white	June	✓		silvered leaves	
Leucojum aestivum 'Gravetye Giant'	500	200	white	April		✓		Good in clay soils
Lilium martagon	2000	150	purple spotted	June		✓		Turks cap lilly
Maianthemum racemosa	700	600	white	April		✓		Rich soil
Monarda 'Scorpion'	800	500	violet	July/Aug		✓		
Monarda 'Squaw'	800	500	scarlet	July/Aug		✓		
Mukdenia rossi	400	300	white	April		✓		
Nectoscordum siculum subsp. Bulgaricum	1000	100	cream/green, flushed purple	June		✓		Spear pointed flower buds; Great under trees

PLANT NAME	Height mm	Spread mm	Flower colour	Scent	Month of Flowering	Evergreen	Deciduous	Leaf Interest	COMMENTS
Nepeta govaniana	600	300	lemon yellow	✓	Aug/Sept		✓	lemon secented foliage	
Omphalodes cappadoccia 'Cherry Ingram'	150	200	blue		April		✓		
Pachysandra procumbens	200	300	white/pink anthers	✓		✓			Flowers smell of spice
Papaver orientale 'Patty's Plum'	700	700	crushed blackcurrant		May		✓		
Persicaria bistorta 'Superba'	900	800	pink		June		✓		
Phlox divaricata 'May Breeze'	200	200	white	✓	May		✓		
Phlox paniculata 'Rosa Pastel'	600	600	pink	✓	July–Sept		✓	dark foliage	
Phlox paniculata 'White Admiral'	900	700	white	✓	July–Sept		✓		
Polemonium caeruleum	600	400	blue		June/July		✓		Jacobs Ladder
Polygonatum hybridum 'Betberg'	1000	700	cream with green tips	✓	April		✓	chocolate foliage	Black berries
Polygonatum odoratum	700	600	cream with green tips	✓	April		✓		Strong scent
Pulmonaria 'Blue Ensign'	300	300	gentian blue		March		✓	dark green foliage	
Pulmonaria officinalis 'Sissinghurst White'	300	300	white		March		✓	white spotted	
Ranunculus aconitifolius 'Flore Pleno'	600	600	double white		May		✓		
Ranunculus acris 'Flore Pleno'	700	600	yellow		May		✓		

Rheum 'Ace of Hearts'	1000	1000	cream	June	✓	
Sanguisorba tenuifolia	700	600	pink/red	June	✓	
Saxifraga rufescens	300	200	cream	June	✓	
Saxifraga stolonifera 'Kinki Purple'	300	250	white	Aug/Sept	✓	
Smyrnium perfoliatum	800	200	acid green/yellow	May	✓	Tri-annual
Speirantha convallarioides	200	300	white	May	✓	
Symphytum ibericum	300	600	white	April	✓	Burnt orange flower buds / Stoloniferous
Tellima grandiflora odorata	600	250	lime green	June	✓	
Tiarella 'Pink Bouquet'	300	250	pink	April/May	✓	
Trachystemon orientalis	500	700	blue/white	March	✓	Dense ground cover
Uvularia grandiflora var. pallida	400	300	lemon yellow	April	✓	
Viola labradorica	150	200	light purple	April	✓	Good ground cover between shrubs
Viola odorata 'Perle Rose'	100	150	pink	April	✓	
Viola odorata sulphurea	100	150	amber	April	✓	
Ferns						
Asplenium scolopendrium 'Cristatum'	300	300	crinkled		✓	Retentive soil
Polystichum setiferum 'Divisilobum Group Herrenhausen'	800	1000			✓	Dry shade

PERENNIALS
Semi-shade Tolerant Perennials for Sandy Soils

PLANT NAME	Height mm	Spread mm	Flower colour	Scent	Month of Flowering	Evergreen	Deciduous	Leaf Interest	COMMENTS
Acanthus mollis	1200	1200	mauve/white		July/Aug		✓	large, broadly cut	Flowering better in full sun
Allium christophii	500	200	lilac		June		✓		
Allium hollandicum 'Purple Sensation'	600	200	lilac/purple		May		✓		
Anemone hupehensis 'September Charm'	800	800	single pink		Aug-Oct		✓		Stoloniferous good ground cover
Anemone nemorosa 'Parlez Vous'	100	150	pale blue		April		✓		Dies down in June
Anemone sylvestris	400	400	white satin		May		✓		Stoloniferous, good ground cover
Anemone × hybrida 'Pamina'	700	700	double pink		Aug-Oct		✓		Stoloniferous good ground cover
Anemone × hybrida 'Whirlwind'	800	800	semi-double white		Aug-Oct		✓		Stoloniferous good ground cover
Arisaema sikokianum	400	300	purple/white		May		✓		One of the best
Arisarum proboscideum	100	100	white/brown		April		✓		Long brown 'mouse' tails; Dies down in summer
Arum italicum spp. *italicum* 'Marmoratum'	200	200	white		April		✓	leaves marbled with cream	Red berries in summer/autumn; Dies down in June
Asplenum scolopendrium	300	300				✓			Native hearts tongue fern
Bergenia 'Overture'	300	300	deep magenta		Mar/April	✓		red foliage in winter	
Brunnera 'Betty Bowring'	500	500	white		April		✓		

Plant			Colour	Flowering			Foliage	Notes
Brunnera 'Jack Frost'	500	500	blue	April		✓	silver leaves/green edge	
Convallaria majalis	150	150	white	April	✓	✓		Lily of the valley
Convallaria majalis 'Albostriata'	150	150	white	April	✓	✓		
Cyclamen coum	100	100	cerise-white	Feb/March		✓		
Cyclamen hederifolium	100	100	pink-white	Aug–Oct		✓	silvered/marbled	
Dicentra formosa	400	400	pink	April/May		✓		Good ground cover between shrubs
Dicentra spectablis	700	600	pink	April/May		✓		Rich soil
Dicentra spectablis 'Alba'	700	600	alba	April/May		✓		Rich soil
Digitalis mertonensis	800	500	dusky rose	June/July		✓		Biennial
Digitalis purpurea 'Apricot'	800	800	apricot	May		✓		Biennial
Disporopsis pernyi	400	300	white	June	✓	✓		
Epimedium grandiflorum 'Lilafee'	400	400	purple	April		✓	purple flushed	
Epimedium perralchicum 'Frohnleiten'	200	600	yellow	April		✓	red tinted foliage	Stoloniferous dry shade
Epimedium versicolor 'Sulphureum'	400	600	yellow	April		✓		Stoloniferous dry shade
Euphorbia amygdaloides 'Purpurea'	400	200	acid yellow/green	April		✓		
Euphorbia griffithii 'Dixter'	600	600	chestnut-tan	June		✓		
Fragaria vesca 'Variegata'	150	500	white	May		✓	striking variegated	Stoloniferous good ground cover between shrubs / Alpine strawberries edible
Galanthus elwesii	150	200	white	Jan–April		✓		
Galanthus nivalis	100	200	white	Jan–April		✓		

PLANT NAME	Height mm	Spread mm	Flower colour	Scent	Month of Flowering	Evergreen	Deciduous	Leaf Interest	COMMENTS
Geranium cantabrigiense 'Cambridge'	300	500	mauve		May		✓	scented	
Geranium himalayense 'Plenum'	200	200	double lilac				✓		
Geranium macrorrhizum album	500	500	off white		May	✓		scented leaf	
Geranium macrorrhizum 'Bevan's Variety'	500	500	magenta pink		May	✓		scented leaf	
Geranium 'Patrica'	600	700	magenta pink/indigo eye		June/July		✓		More compact than G.psilostemon
Geranium phaeum 'Samobor'	800	700	purple		June		✓	chocolate blotched	
Gillenia trifoliata	700	700	white blush pink		June		✓		
Helleborus 'Winter Moonbeam'	400	400	pink buds cream flowers		Feb/Apr	✓		marbled foliage	Flower colour matures to deep red
Helleborus 'Winter Sunshine'	400	400	pink buds cream flowers			✓		dark green foliage	Flower colour matures to deep red
Heuchera 'Midnight Rose'	250	250	pink		June	✓		red speckled black/red leaves	
Iris japonica 'Variegata'	600	600	blue/yellow/white		May	✓		boldly variegated leaves	
Lamium 'White Nancy'	150	150	white		June	✓		silvered leaves	
Leucojum aestivum 'Gravetye Giant'	500	200	white		April		✓		Good in clay soils
Leucojum vernum	200	200	white		Feb/March		✓		Good in clay soils
Lilium martagon	2000	150	purple spotted		June		✓		Turks cap lily

Nectoscordum siculum subsp. *Bulgaricum*	1000	100	cream/green flushed purple	June	✓			Spear pointed flower buds / Great under trees
Nepeta govaniana	600	300	lemon yellow	Aug/Sept	✓		lemon scented foliage	
Pachysandra procumbens	200	300	white/pink anthers			✓		Flowers smell of spice
Papaver orientale 'Helen Elizabeth'	700	700	satin pink	May	✓			
Phlox divicarta subsp. *Laphamii* 'Chattahoochee'	150	200	lilac	May	✓	✓		
Polemonium caeruleum	600	400	blue	June/July	✓			Jacobs Ladder
Primula Seiboldii 'Pago-Pago'	150	200	white/pink/carmine	May	✓			Mixed colours
Pulmonaria 'Blue Ensign'	300	300	gentian blue	March	✓		dark green foliage	
Pulmonaria officinalis 'Sissinghurst White'	300	300	white	March	✓		white spotted	
Saxifraga rufescens	300	200	cream	June	✓			
Saxifraga stolonifera 'Kinki Purple'	300	250	white	Aug/Sept	✓			
Speirantha convallarioides	200	300	white	May	✓	✓		
Tellima grandiflora odorata	600	250	lime green	June	✓	✓		
Thalictrum delavayi album	700	300	white	July/August	✓			
Thalictrum delavayi 'Hewitt's Double'	1200	500	mauve	August	✓			
Tiarella 'Pink Bouquet'	300	250	pink	April/May	✓			
Uvularia grandiflora var. *pallida*	400	300	lemon yellow	April	✓			
Viola 'Governor Herrick'	200	200	large blue	April/May	✓			

PLANT NAME	Height mm	Spread mm	Flower colour	Scent	Month of Flowering	Evergreen	Deciduous	Leaf Interest	COMMENTS
Viola odorata 'Perle Rose'	100	150	pink	✓	April		✓		
Viola odorata sulphurea	100	150	amber	✓	April		✓		
Ferns									
Asplenum scolopendrium 'Cristatum'	300	300				✓		crinkled	Retentive soil
Polystichum seteriferum 'Divisilobum Group Herrenhausen'	800	1000					✓		Dry shade

PERENNIALS
Sun Loving Perennials for Clay/Loam Soils

PLANT NAME	Height mm	Spread mm	Flower colour	Scent	Month of Flowering	Evergreen	Deciduous	Leaf Interest	COMMENTS
Acanthus spinosus	1000	1000	mauve/white		July/Aug		✓	glossy, deep cut	
Alchemilla mollis	250	250	green		July/August		✓		
Allium 'Globemaster'	20000	200	soft lilac		May		✓		
Allium hollandicum 'Purple Sensation'	600	200	lilac/purple		May		✓		
Amsonia tabernaemontana	500	500	lilac		June		✓		
Anemone sylvestris	400	400	white satin		May		✓		Stoloniferous, good ground cover
Aquilega vulgaris 'William Guinness'	500	200	black/maroon/white		June		✓		
Artemisia lactiflora 'Guizhou Group'	1200	500	white		July/August		✓		
Artemisia ludiviciana 'Valerie Finnis'	700	400	silver		June		✓		
Asphodeline lutea	900	500	yellow		June		✓		
Aster amellus 'Veilchenkonigen'	500	300	violet		Sept/Oct		✓		
Aster frikartii 'Monch'	900	600	blue		July/August		✓		
Aster 'Little Carlow'	1200	600	blue		Sept/Oct		✓		
Aster novae-anglaie 'Andenken an Alma Potschke'	1000	700	cherry-red		Sept/Oct		✓		
Astrantia major 'Buckland'	700	400	dusky pink		June/July		✓		

PLANT NAME	Height mm	Spread mm	Flower colour	Scent	Month of Flowering	Evergreen	Deciduous	Leaf Interest	COMMENTS
Astrantia major 'Hadspen Blood'	600	500	blood red		June/July		✓		
Astrantia major 'Roma'	650	400	deep pink		May-July		✓		
Bergenia 'Overture'	300	300	deep magenta		Mar/April	✓	✓		red foliage in winter
Calamagrostis × acutiflora 'Karl Foerster'	1400	800	amber		July-Dec	✓			
Calamintha subsp. nepeta 'Blue Cloud'	300	300	blue		July/Aug		✓		
Campanula punctata 'Rubrifolia'	600	400	pink		June/July		✓		Stoloniferous red stems
Campanula rupestris 'Sarastro'	700	600	blue		June/July		✓		
Campanula takesimana 'Elizabeth'	300	300	pink		June/July		✓		
Carex buchananii	500	500				✓			bronze foliage
Cephalaria gigantea	2000	500	primrose yellow		July/August		✓		
Chaerophyllum angustifolium 'Album'	700	600	white		June/July		✓	✓	
Chelone obliqua	800	400	pink		Aug/Sept		✓		
Cirsium rivule 'Atropurpureum'	1800	700	red		May/June		✓		
Clematis integrifolia	500	500	blue		June		✓		no tall support necessary
Crocosmia × crocosmiiflora 'Gerbe d'Oro'	600	300	apricot		August		✓		attractive bronze leaves

Name	Height	Spread	Colour	Flowering	✓	Notes
Crocosmia × crocosmiiflora 'Honey Angels'	600	300	yellow	August	✓	
Crocosmia × crocosmiiflora 'Lucifer'	1100	500	red	July/August	✓	
Dahlia 'Bishop of Llandaff'	850	500	scarlet	July–Nov	✓	black/maroon foliage
Dahlia 'Twynings After Eight'	1000	600	white	July–Nov	✓	almost black foliage
Dictamnus albus purpureus	600	300	mauve veined purple	August	✓	
Dierama 'Merlin'	1000	500	blackberry purple	August	✓	
Digitalis mertonensis	800	500	dusky rose	June/July	✓	Biennial
Digitalis purpurea f. albiflora	1000	500	white	May	✓	Biennial
Echinacea hybrida 'Fatal Attraction'	600	600	purple–pink horizontal	July–Nov	✓	
Echinacea purpurea 'Magnus'	1000	7000	deep mauve	July–Nov	✓	
Echinacea purpurea 'Ruby Giant'	1000	750	ruby red ✓	July–Nov	✓	
Echinops ritro 'Veitch's Blue'	800	500	blue	July–Nov	✓	
Eryngium alpinum	700	400	metallic blue	June/July	✓	
Eryngium bourgatii 'Graham Stuart Thomas'	600	400	violet–blue	June/July	✓	variegated foliage
Eryngium × tripartitum	600	400	deep blue	August	✓	
Eupatorium maculatum 'Atropurpureum'	1800	700	rose–purple	August	✓	
Eupatorium rugosum 'Chocolate'	1200	700	white	Oct	✓	chocolate foliage
Euphorbia characias 'Blue Wonder'	500	400	silver–blue bracts	June	✓ ✓	blue foliage
Euphorbia characias Wulfenii	1100	700	lime–green	March/April	✓	

PLANT NAME	Height mm	Spread mm	Flower colour	Scent	Month of Flowering	Evergreen	Deciduous	Leaf Interest	COMMENTS
Euphorbia griffithii 'Dixter'	800	700	burnt red bracts		June		✓	chestnut -tan foliage	
Euphorbia polychroma	250	250	yellow		April		✓		
Francoa sonchifolia 'Rogerson's form'	500	250	multicoloured		July		✓		
Galtonia candicans	1000	150	white		July/Aug		✓		
Geranium clarkei 'Kashmir White'	300	500	white lilac veins		May		✓		
Geranium 'Elke'	120	250	dusky pink		June-Sept				
Geranium himalayense 'Plenum'	200	200	double lilac				✓		
Geranium macrorrhizum album	500	500	off white		May	✓		scented leaf	
Geranium macrorrhizum 'Bevan's Variety'	500	500	magenta pink		May	✓		scented leaf	
Geranium 'Patrica'	600	700	magenta pink/indigo eye		June/July		✓		More compact than G.psilostemon
Geranium phaeum 'Samobor'	800	700	purple		June		✓	chocolate blotched	
Geranium sanginium album	120	250	white		June		✓		
Helenium 'Butterpat'	900	600	yellow		August		✓		
Helenium 'Indianersommer'	900	600	orange-red		Sept		✓	late flowering -Sept	
Helenium 'Moerheim Beauty'	900	600	rusty brown		July-Nov		✓		
Helenium 'Ruby Tuesday'	1000	600	ruby-red		August		✓		
Helenium 'Sahins Early Flowerer'	800	600	streaked orange		July-Sept		✓		
Helenium 'Wyndley'	800	600	bronze and yellow		July-Sept		✓		

Plant			Flower colour	Flowering			Notes
Helleborus hybridus	400	600	white-black	Jan-April	✓		Flower colour in all shades
Helleborus 'Winter Moonbeam'	400	400	pink buds cream flowers	Feb/Apr	✓	marbled foliage	Flower colour matures to deep red
Helleborus 'Winter Sunshine'	400	400	pink buds cream flowers	Feb/Apr	✓	dark green foliage	Flower colour matures to deep red
Hemerocallis 'American Revolution'	700	600	almost black	July	✓		
Hemerocallis 'Anzac'	600	600	deep red, golden yellow throat	July	✓		
Heuchera 'Midnight Rose'	250	250	pink	June	✓	red speckled, black/red leaves	
Heuchera 'Obsidian'	300	300	white	June	✓		
Iris 'Cherry Garden'	300	300	red	May	✓		
Iris ensta 'Innocence'	800	800	double white	July	✓		Boggy soil/ shallow water
Iris 'Green Spot'	300	300	white /green	May	✓		
Iris siberica 'Butter and Sugar'	800	700	yellow and cream	June	✓		
Iris unguicularis	300	300	blue	Feb/Mar	✓		Sheltered position
Kniphofia 'Percy's Pride'	1000	800	green buds opening white	September	✓		
Lamium 'White Nancy'	150	150	white	June	✓	silvered leaves	
Lavandula 'Hidcote'	250	350	dark blue	June-Aug	✓		Compact good for hedges
Lavandula 'Munsted Blue'	300	350	blue	June-Aug	✓		Compact good for hedges
Leucanthemum × *superbum* 'Aglaia'	600	600	white	July-Sept	✓ ✓		Frilly double flowers
Leucanthemum × *superbum* 'Goldrausch'	800	700	cream	July-Sept	✓		
Leucojum aestivum 'Gravetye Giant'	500	200	white	April	✓		Good in clay soils
Leucojum vernum	100	100	white/ yellow tips	Feb/Mar	✓		Good in clay soils

PLANT NAME	Height mm	Spread mm	Flower colour	Scent	Month of Flowering	Evergreen	Deciduous	Leaf Interest	COMMENTS
Lilirope muscari	400	300	violet-blue		Aug/Sept		✓		
Lysimachia ephemerum	800	700	white		July/August		✓		glaucous foliage
Lythrum salicaria 'Robert'	800	700	cerise pink		July/August		✓		
Miscanthus sinensis 'Flamingo'	1300	1000	rose-pink		Sept-Dec	✓			Red stems
Miscanthus sinensis 'Kleine Silberspinne'	1000	750	silver		Sept-Dec	✓			
Monarda 'Scorpion'	800	500	violet	✓	July/Aug		✓		
Nepeta sibirica 'Souvenir d'Andre Chaudron'	400	500	blue		June-Aug		✓		
Nepeta subsessilis	700	700	blue		June		✓		
Origanum laevigatum 'Hopleys'	450	400	rose-pink		August/Sept	✓			
Panicum virgatum 'Warrior'	1300	1300	pale pink		Sept-Dec	✓			bronze flushed
Papaver orientale 'Helen Elizabeth'	700	700	satin pink		May		✓		
Pennisetum alopecuroides 'Hameln'	700	600	red edge		Sept-Dec	✓			caterpillar-like flower heads
Penstemon 'Andenken an Fredrich Hahn'	750	600	garnet-red		July-Oct	✓			Reliably tough
Penstemon 'Rich Ruby'	600	600	ruby-red		July-Oct		✓		
Phlomis tuberosa 'Amazone'	120	700	rosey pink		June		✓		
Phlox paniculata 'Rosa Pastell'	600	600	pink	✓	July-Sept		✓		dark foliage
Physostegia virginiana 'Rose Bouquet'	80	700	rosey pink		August/Sept	✓			

Plant	Height	Spread	Flower colour	Flowering period	✓	Foliage	Notes
Polygonatum × hybridum 'Betberg'	1000	700	cream with green tips	April	✓	chocolate foliage	Black berries
Polygonatum hybridum 'Striatum'	600	600	cream with green tips	April	✓	bold variegation	
Polygonatum odoratum var. *pluriflorum* 'Variegatum'	700	600	cream with green tips	April	✓	cream edge to leaves	Pink shoots and stems
Rudbeckia fulgida var. *speciosa* 'Goldsturm'	600	600	deep yellow black eyed	Aug-Sept	✓		
Salvia nemerosa 'Ostfriesland'	450	450	violet-blue	July-Sept	✓		Compact
Salvia × sylvestris 'Mainacht'	500	500	deep blue	June-Aug	✓		Aromatic foliage
Sanguisorba tenuifolia	700	600	pink/red	June	✓		
Scabiosa caucasica 'Miss Willmott'	700	500	white	June-Sept	✓		
Scabiosa columbaria var. *ochroleuca*	700	700	lemon yellow	Aug-Nov	✓		
Scabiosa gigantea	2000	600	lemon yellow	Aug-Nov	✓		
Schizostylis coccinea 'Maiden's Blush'	500	500	pale pink	Sept-Dec	✓		
Schizostylis coccinea 'Major'	550	550	red	Sept-Dec	✓		
Sedum 'Purple Emperor'	600	500	dark red	Aug-Nov	✓	dark foliage	
Sedum spectabile 'Iceberg'	600	500	white	Aug-Nov	✓		
Stipa gigantea	2000	1000	golden oats	June-Dec	✓		
Stipa tenuissima	300	300	soft green	May-July	✓	feathery foliage	
Trifolium ochroleucon	700	700	pale yellow	June/July	✓		
Valeriana phu 'Aurea'	700	600	white	June/July	✓		Yellow spring foliage
Verbascum chaxii 'Album'	800	600	white	July/August	✓		
Veronica gentianoides	500	400	pale blue	May	✓		
Veronicastrum virginicum album	1100	800	white	October	✓		

PERENNIALS
Sun Loving Perennials for Sandy Soils

PLANT NAME	Height mm	Spread mm	Flower colour	Scent	Month of Flowering	Evergreen	Deciduous	Leaf Interest	COMMENTS
Acanthus spinosus	1000	1000	mauve/white		July/Aug		✓	glossy, deep cut	
Alchemilla mollis	250	250	green		July/August		✓		
Allium christophii	500	200	lilac		June		✓		
Allium hollandicum 'Purple Sensation'	600	200	lilac/purple		May		✓		
Anemone sylvestris	400	400	white satin		May		✓		Stoloniferous, good ground cover
Angelica gigas	2000	750	ruby		July/Aug		✓		Monocarpic
Anthemis punctata subsp. *Cupaniana*	200	300	white		July		✓		
Anthemis 'Sauce Hollandaise'	300	300	rich cream		August		✓		
Aquilegia vulgaris 'William Guinness'	500	200	black/maroon/ white		June		✓		
Artemisia absinthium 'Lambrook Silver'	500	500	yellow		July/August		✓		
Aster amellus 'Veilchenkonigen'	500	300			Sept/Oct		✓		
Bergenia 'Bressingham White'	300	300	white		Mar/April		✓		
Calamintha nepeta subsp. 'Blue Cloud'	300	300	blue		July/Aug		✓		
Delphinium 'Galahad'	1500	500	white		June		✓		
Dictamnus albus	600	300	white veined purple		August		✓		burning bush

Name			Colour	Flowering	✓	Notes
Dierama 'Merlin'	1000	500	blackberry purple	August	✓	
Digitalis purpurea f. albiflora	1000	500	white	May	✓	Biennial
Digitalis purpurea 'Apricot'	800	800	apricot	May	✓	Biennial
Echinops ritro 'Veitch's Blue'	800	500	blue	July-Nov	✓	
Eryngium alpinum	700	400	metallic blue	June/July	✓	
Eryngium bourgatii 'Graham Stuart Thomas'	600	400	violet-blue	June/July	✓	variegated foliage
Erysimum 'Bowles Mauve'	700	500	lilac	May-Sept	✓	
Euphorbia characias 'Wulfenii'	1100	700	lime-green	March/ April	✓	
Euphorbia polychroma	250	250	yellow bracts	April	✓	
Euphorbia × *martinii*	800	800	lime bracts	March	✓	red stems
Francoa sonchifolia 'Rogerson's form'	500	250	multicoloured	July	✓	
Galtonia candidans	1000	150	white	July/Aug	✓	
Geranium cantabrigiense 'Cambridge'	300	500	mauve	May	✓	scented
Geranium 'Elke'	120	250	dusky pink	June-Sept	✓	
Geranium himalayense 'Plenum'	200	200	double lilac	June	✓	
Geranium macrorrhizum 'Ingwersen's variety'	500	500	pale pink	May	✓	scented leaf / Stoloniferous
Geranium maculatum 'Chatto'	400	400	pink		✓	Early
Geranium phaeum 'Samobor'	800	700	purple	June	✓	chocolate blotched
Geranium psilostemon	700	800	magenta pink	June/July	✓	Rambling
Geranium sanginium album	120	250	white	June	✓	
Geranium sanginium var. *striatum*	120	250	pink	June-Sept	✓	
Helleborus hybridus	400	600	white-black	Jan-April	✓	Flower colour in all shades

PLANT NAME	Height mm	Spread mm	Flower colour	Scent	Month of Flowering	Evergreen	Deciduous	Leaf Interest	COMMENTS
Helleborus 'Winter Moonbeam'	400	400	pink buds cream flowers		Feb/Apr	✓		marbled foliage	Flower colour matures to deep red
Helleborus 'Winter Sunshine'	400	400	pink buds cream flowers			✓		dark green foliage	Flower colour matures to deep red
Heuchera 'Chocolate Ruffles'	300	300	white		June	✓		chocolate crinkled leaves	
Heuchera 'Obsidian'	300	300	white		June	✓			
Iris 'Action Front'	800	800	copper-red		June		✓		
Iris 'Deep Black'	700	800	almost black		June		✓		
Iris robusta 'Gerald Darby'	900	800	deep blue		June		✓	dark blue stain at base of leaves	
Iris sibirica 'Tropic Night'	700	600	deep blue		June		✓		
Iris sibirica 'White Swirl'	800	700	white		May		✓		
Iris unguicularis	300	300	blue		Feb/Mar		✓		Sheltered position
Kniphofia 'Brimstone'	700	700	yellow		June/July		✓		
Kniphofia 'Nancy's Red'	600	600	red		June/July		✓		
Kniphofia 'Timothy'	1000	800	orange		July		✓		
Lamium 'White Nancy'	150	150	white		June	✓		silvered leaves	
Lavandula 'Hidcote'	250	350	dark blue		June-Aug	✓			Compact good for hedges
Leucojum autumnale	100	100	white		Aug/Sept		✓		
Libertia grandiflora	500	500	white		May/June	✓			
Liriope muscari 'Variegata'	400	300	violet-blue		Aug/Sept		✓		Cream variegated foliage
Lythrum salicaria 'Blush'	800	700	blush pink		July/August		✓		

Plant			Colour	Flowering	✓	Notes
Nepeta sibirica 'Souvenir d'Andre Chaudron'	400	500	blue	June-Aug	✓	
Nepeta 'Six Hills Giant'	600	500	blue	June-Sept	✓	
Origanum laevigatum 'Hopleys'	450	400	rose-pink	August/Sept ✓		
Papaver orientale 'Patty's Plum'	700	700	crushed blackcurrant	May	✓	
Penstemon 'Apple Blossom'	600	500	pale pink	July-Oct	✓	
Penstemon 'Drinkstone Red'	700	600	bright red	July-Oct	✓	
Penstemon 'Rich Ruby'	600	600	ruby-red	July-Oct	✓	
Penstemon 'White Bedder'	700	600	white	July/August	✓	
Phlox paniculata 'Rosa Pastell'	600	600	pink	✓ July-Sept	✓	dark foliage
Salvia guaranitica 'Blue Enigma'	800	700	deep blue	Sept	✓	
Salvia nemerosa 'Ostfriesland'	450	450	violet-blue	July-Sept	✓	Compact
Salvia x sylvestris 'Mainacht'	500	500	deep blue	June-Aug	✓	Aromatic foliage
Scabiosa caucasica 'Blue Seal'	700	500	blue	June-Sept	✓	
Scabiosa caucasica 'Miss Willmott'	700	500	white	June-Sept	✓	
Scabiosa columbaria var. *ochroleuca*	700	700	lemon yellow	Aug- Nov	✓	
Scabiosa gigantea	2000	600	lemon yellow	Aug- Nov	✓	
Schizostylis coccinea 'Maiden's Blush'	500	500	pale pink	Sept-Dec	✓	
Schizostylis coccinea 'Major'	550	550	red	Sept-Dec	✓	
Sedum 'Herbstfreude'	600	500	pink	Aug-Nov	✓	
Sedum 'Munsted Red'	600	500	red	Aug-Nov	✓	
Sidalcea 'Brilliant'	700	600	pink	July/August	✓	

PLANT NAME	Height mm	Spread mm	Flower colour	Scent	Month of Flowering	Evergreen	Deciduous	Leaf Interest	COMMENTS
Sidalcea 'Elsie Heugh'	800	600	satin pink		July/August		✓		
Thermopsis lupinoides	700	500	yellow		April		✓	black stems	
Tradescantia hybrida 'Zwanenburg Blue'	450	450	beep blue				✓		
Trifolium ochroleucon	700	700	pale yellow		June/July		✓		
Tulbaghia violacea alba	500	250	white		May-Nov		✓		
Valariana phu 'Aurea'	700	600	white		June/July		✓		Yellow spring foliage
Verbascum chaxii 'Album'	800	600	white		July/August		✓		
Grasses									
Calamagrostis acutiflora 'Karl Foerster'	1400	800	amber		July-Dec	✓			
Carex buchananii	500	500				✓		bronze foliage	
Miscanthus sinensis 'Flamingo'	1300	1000	rose-pink		Sept-Dec	✓			Red stems
Miscanthus sinensis 'Kleine Fontaine'	1300	1000	amber		Sept-Dec	✓		white veined	
Miscanthus sinensis 'Yakushima Dwarf'	1000	750	pink		Sept-Dec	✓		grey leaves	Good autumn colour
Panicum virgatum 'Warrior'	1300	1300	pale pink		Sept-Dec	✓		bronze flushed	
Pennisetum alopecuroides 'Hameln'	700	600	red edge		Sept-Dec	✓			Caterpillar-like flower heads
Stipa gigantea	2000	1000	golden oats		June-Dec	✓			
Stipa tenuissima	300	300	soft green		May-July	✓		feathery foliage	

PERENNIALS

To attract Bees and Butterflies

PLANT NAME	Height mm	Spread mm	Flower colour	Scent	Month of Flowering	Evergreen	Deciduous	Leaf Interest	COMMENTS
Allium christophii	500	200	lilac		June		✓		
Allium hollandicum 'Purple Sensation'	600	200	lilac/purple		May		✓		
Anemone hybrida 'Honorine Jobert'	700	700	white		August/Sept	✓		single varieties	
Anemone hybrida 'September Charm'	600	600	pink		August/Sept	✓			
Angelica gigas	2000	750	ruby		July/Aug		✓		Monocarpic
Aster amellus 'King George'	700	500	violet/blue		Sept		✓		
Aster frikartii 'Monch'	900	600	blue		July/August		✓		
Aster laterifolius 'Prince'	1000	700	pink		Sept/Nov		✓		
Aster novae-angliae 'Andenken an Alma Potschke'	1000	700	cherry-red		Sept/Oct		✓		
Astrantia major 'Hadspen Blood'	600	500	blood-red		June/July		✓		
Astrantia major 'Roma'	650	400	deep pink		June/July		✓		
Calamintha subsp. *nepeta* 'Blue Cloud'	300	300	blue		July/Aug		✓		
Cephalaria gigantea	2000	500	primrose yellow		July/August		✓		
Ceratostigma plumbaginoides	300	200	colbalt-blue		Sept/October	✓			

PLANT NAME	Height mm	Spread mm	Flower colour	Scent	Month of Flowering	Evergreen	Deciduous	Leaf Interest	COMMENTS
Clematis integrifolia	500	500	blue		June		✓		no tall support necessary
Dahlia 'Twynings After Eight'	1000	600	white		July-Nov		✓		almost black foliage
Delphinium Pacific hybrids	1200	500	various		June		✓		
Dictamnus albus purpureus	600	300	mauve veined purple		August		✓		
Digitalis purpurea f. albiflora	1000	500	white		May		✓		Biennial
Echinacea hybrida 'Fatal Attraction'	600	600	purple-pink horizontal		July-Nov		✓		
Echinacea purpurea 'Kim's Mophead'	450	450	white		July-Nov		✓		
Echinacea purpurea 'Ruby Giant'	1000	750	ruby red	✓	July-Nov		✓		
Echinacea purpurea 'White Swan'	700	600	white		July-Nov		✓		
Echinops ritro 'Veitch's Blue'	800	500	blue		July-Nov		✓		
Eryngium planum 'Blaukappe'	700	400	deep blue		August		✓		
Eryngium × oliverianum	600	400	deep blue		June/Sept		✓		
Eupatorium maculatum 'Atropurpureum'	1800	700	rose-purple		August		✓		
Francoa sonchifolia 'Rogerson's form'	500	250	multicoloured		July		✓		
Galanthus elwesii	200	160	white		Feb		✓		
Galanthus nivalis	150	150	white		Feb		✓		
Galtonia candidans	1000	150	white		July/Aug		✓		
Geranium cantabrigiense 'Cambridge'	300	500	mauve		May		✓		scented

Plant			Flower colour	Flowering	✓	Foliage/notes	Notes
Geranium 'Dusky Crug'	400	400	pink	May-Dec	✓	chocolate-maroon	
Geranium 'Elke'	120	250	dusky pink	June-Sept	✓		
Geranium himalayense 'Plenum'	200	200	double lilac	June	✓		
Geranium macrorrhizum album	500	500	off white	May	✓	scented leaf	
Geranium 'Patrica'	600	700	magenta pink/indigo eye	June/July	✓		More compact than *G. psilostemon*
Geranium phaeum 'Samobor'	800	700	purple	June	✓	chocolate blotched	
Geranium 'Salome'	400	400	dusky pink/veined dark violet	July/Sept	✓		
Geranium sanginium var. striatum	120	250	pink	June-Sept	✓		
Geranium 'Tanya Rendall'	200	200	cerise	July-Oct	✓	deep-green/bronze	
Geum 'Lionel Cox'	200	200	lemon-yellow/apricot	April	✓		
Gillenia trifoliata	700	700	white blush pink	June	✓		
Helianthus 'Lemon Queen'	2000	2000	yellow	August-October	✓		
Helenium 'Butterpat'	900	600	yellow	August	✓		
Helenium 'Moerheim Beauty'	900	600	rusty brown	July-Nov	✓		
Helenium 'Waldraut'	800	600	brown-red /yellow	July-Sept	✓		
Helleborus hybridus	400	600	white-black	Jan-April	✓		Flower colour in all shades
Helleborus 'Winter Moonbeam'	400	400	pink buds cream flowers	Feb/Apr	✓	marbled foliage	Flower colour matures to deep red
Helleborus 'Winter Sunshine'	400	400	pink buds cream flowers	Feb/Apr	✓	dark green foliage	Flower colour matures to deep red
Kniphofia 'Nancy's Red'	600	600	red	June/July	✓		
Kniphofia 'Percy's Pride'	1000	800	green buds opening white	September	✓		

PLANT NAME	Height mm	Spread mm	Flower colour	Scent	Month of Flowering	Evergreen	Deciduous	Leaf Interest	COMMENTS
Lamium 'White Nancy'	150	150	white		June	✓		silvered leaves	
Lavandula 'Hidcote'	250	350	dark blue		June-Aug	✓			Compact good for hedges
Leucojum aestivum 'Gravetye Giant'	500	200	white		April		✓		Good in clay soils
Libertia grandiflora	500	500	white		May/June	✓			
Lythrum salicaria 'Robert'	800	700	cerise pink		July/August		✓		
Monarda 'Scorpion'	800	500	violet	✓	July/Aug		✓		
Monarda 'Squaw'	800	500	scarlet	✓	July/Aug		✓		
Nepeta sibirica 'Souvenir d'Andre Chaudron'	400	500	blue	✓	June-Aug		✓		
Origanum laevigatum 'Hopleys'	450	400	rose-pink		August/Sept	✓			
Papaver orientale 'Helen Elizabeth'	700	700	satin pink		May		✓		
Penstemon 'Andenken an' Fredrich Hahn	750	600	garnet-red		July-Oct		✓		Reliably tough
Penstemon 'Apple Blossom'	600	600	pale pink		July-Oct		✓		
Penstemon 'Sour Grapes'	600	600	blue		July-Oct		✓		
Penstemon 'White Bedder'	700	600	white		July/August		✓		
Phlomis tuberosa 'Amazone'	120	700	rosey pink		June		✓		
Phlox paniculata 'Sky Light'	900	700	lavender	✓	July-Sept		✓		
Phlox paniculata 'White Admiral'	900	700	white	✓	July-Sept		✓		

					✓	
Physostegia virginiana 'Summer Spire'	80	700	rosey pink	August/Sept		
Primula florindae	1000	500	yellow	July	✓	Candelabra primula
Primula japonica alba	600	300	white	May	✓	Candelabra primula
Primula japonica 'Millers Crimson'	600	300	rich pink	May	✓	Candelabra primula
Primula 'Oriental Sunrise'	400	300	mixed shades	June	✓	Candelabra primula
Primula pulverulenta	400	300	cerise to wine red	June	✓	Candelabra primula
Primula seiboldii 'Pago-Pago'	150	150	mixed shades	May	✓	Candelabra primula
Primula veris	175	175	yellow	April	✓	
Primula vulgaris	140	150	yellow	March–May	✓	
Rudbeckia fulgida var. speciosa 'Goldsturm'	600	600	deep yellow black eyed	Aug–Sept	✓	
Salvia guaranitica 'Blue Enigma'	800	700	deep blue	Sept	✓	
Salvia nemerosa 'Lubecca'	600	600	violet-blue	July–Sept	✓	
Salvia × sylvestris 'Mainacht'	500	500	deep blue	June–Aug	✓	Aromatic foliage
Sanguisorba tenuifolia	700	600	pink/red	June	✓	
Scabiosa caucasica 'Blue Seal'	700	500	blue	June–Sept	✓	
Scabiosa columbaria var. ochroleuca	700	700	lemon yellow	Aug–Nov	✓	
Scabiosa gigantea	2000	600	lemon yellow	Aug–Nov	✓	
Schizostylis coccinea 'Jennifer'	500	500	pink	Sept–Dec	✓	
Schizostylis coccinea 'Major'	550	550	red	Sept–Dec	✓	
Schizostylis coccinea 'Mollie Gould'	400	400	shining pink	Sept–Dec	✓	
Sedum 'Mohrchen'	600	500	pink	Aug–Nov	✓	large leaves

PLANT NAME	Height mm	Spread mm	Flower colour	Scent	Month of Flowering	Evergreen	Deciduous	Leaf Interest	COMMENTS
Sedum spectabile 'Iceberg'	600	500	white		Aug-Nov		✓		
Sidalcea 'Elsie Heugh'	800	600	satin-pink		July/Aug		✓		
Thermopsis lupinoides	700	500	yellow		April		✓	black stems	
Trifolium ochroleucon	700	700	pale yellow		June/July		✓		
Tulbaghia violacea	500	250	pink		May-Nov		✓		Warm spot required
Thymus vulgaris	150	250	lilac	✓	June-Sept		✓		
Verbascum chaxii 'Album'	800	600	white		July/August		✓		
Veronica gentianoides	500	400	pale blue		May		✓		
Veronicastrum virginicum 'Apollo'	1100	800	lilac		August		✓		

PERENNIALS

Useful Shrubs Easy to Grow in Most climages (Frosts to Minus 10°C)

PLANT NAME	Height mm	Spread mm	Flower colour	Scent	Month of Flowering	Evergreen	Deciduous	Leaf Interest	COMMENTS
Aesculus parviflora	2200	2000	cream	✓	July		✓		
Abelia grandiflora	2000	2000	pink		Aug/Oct		✓		
Amelanchier lamarckii	4000	3000	white	✓	April		✓		
Buddleia 'Lochinch'	5000	3000	blue	✓	August				
Choysia ternata	2000	2000	white	✓	June–Oct		✓		
Cornus alba 'Siberica'	1700	1700	white		June		✓		Rec stems
Cornus stolonifera 'Flaviramea'	1700	1700	white		June		✓		Yellow green
Corylus avellana 'Contorta'	3000	2000	golden catkins		March		✓	twisted stems	
Corylus maxima 'Purpurea'	3000	3000	pale yellow catkins		March		✓	plum foliage	
Cotinus coggygria 'Royal Purple'	2000	2000	ruby red		August		✓	rich ruby foliage	
Cotoneaster salicifolius	3000	3000	cream		May		✓		Red berries
Deutzia gracillis	1800	1800	pink		May		✓		
Eleagnus pungens 'Maculata'	2000	2000	white	✓	September	✓		variegated foliage	
Euonymus alatus	3000	2000	red		May		✓	red foliage in autumn	Pink berries
Hibiscus 'Blue Bird'	1800	1800	blue		August–Sept	✓			
Hydrangea 'Bluebird'	1500	1500	pink/blue		August–Sept	✓			blue if acid soil
Ilex 'JC Van Toll'	2500	2000	white		May	✓			Red berries

PLANT NAME	Height mm	Spread mm	Flower colour	Scent	Month of Flowering	Evergreen	Deciduous	Leaf Interest	COMMENTS
Kolwitzia amabilis 'Pink Cloud'	3000	3000	pink		May		✓		
Lonicera fragrantissima	2000	1800	cream		Jan–March		✓		
Mahonia 'Winter Sun'	1500	1500	yellow		December	✓			
Osmarea burkwoodii	2500	2500	white	✓	April		✓		Good for hedges
Philadelphus 'Beauclerk'	1500	1500	white	✓	June		✓		
Physocarpus opulifolius 'Diablo'	3000	3000	white		June		✓		
Ribes 'White Icicle'	2500	2000	white	✓	April		✓		Honey scented
Rosa 'Buff Beauty'	2000	2000	apricot	✓	July–August		✓		
Sambucus nigra 'Black Lace'	2500	2000	pink		June		✓	dark foliage	Black edible berries
Syringa microphylla	2000	2000	pink	✓	May–Sept		✓		Sprays of small flowers
Viburnum burkwoodii	2500	2500	cream	✓	April		✓		
Viburnum juddii	1000	1000	white	✓	May		✓		
Viburnum opulus compactum	1500	1500	white		May		✓		Red berries attactive to birds

PERENNIALS
Suitable for Groundcover between Shrubs

PLANT NAME	Height mm	Spread mm	Flower colour	Scent	Month of Flowering	Evergreen	Deciduous	Leaf Interest	COMMENTS
Anemone × hybrida 'Whirlwind'	800	800	semi-double white		Aug-Oct		✓		Stoloniferous good ground cover
Anemone × hybrida 'Pamina'	700	700	double pink		Aug-Oct		✓		Stoloniferous good ground cover
Anemone nemorosa 'Royal Blue'	100	150	mid blue		April		✓		Dies down in June
Anemone ranunculoides	100	150	yellow		April		✓		Dies down in June
Anemone sylvestris	400	400	white satin		May		✓		Stoloniferous, good ground cover
Arisarum proboscideum	100	100	white/brown		April		✓		Long brown 'mouse' tails Dies down in summer
Arum italicum spp. italicum 'Marmoratum'	200	200	white		April		✓	leaves marbled with cream	Red berries in summer/autumn Dies down in June
Asarum arifolium	150	300	red		March	✓			Good ground cover
Brunnera 'Betty Bowring'	500	500	white		April		✓		
Brunnera 'Jack Frost'	500	500	blue		April		✓	silver leaves/green edge	
Campanula punctata 'Rubrifolia'	600	400	pink		June/July		✓		Stoloniferous red stems
Convallaria majalis	150	150	white	✓	April	✓			Lily of the valley
Convallaria majalis var. rosea	150	150	white	✓	April	✓			
Cyclamen coum	100	100	cerise-white		Feb/March		✓		

PLANT NAME	Height mm	Spread mm	Flower colour	Scent	Month of Flowering	Evergreen	Deciduous	Leaf Interest	COMMENTS
Cyclamen hederifolium	100	100	pink-white		Aug–Oct		✓	silvered/marbled	
Dicentra formosa	400	400	pink		April/May		✓		Good ground cover between shrubs
Dicentra 'Langtrees'	600	400	white		April/May		✓	blue/grey	
Dicentra spectablis	700	600	pink		April/May		✓		Rich soil
Dicentra spectablis 'Alba'	700	600	alba		April/May		✓		Rich soil
Disporopsis peryni	400	300	white	✓	June	✓			
Disporum flavens	700	400	yellow		April		✓		
Epimedium grandiflorum 'Lilafee'	400	400	purple		April		✓	purple flushed	
Epimedium × perralchicum 'Frohnleiten'	200	600	yellow		April	✓		red tinted foliage	Stoloniferous dry shade
Epimedium × perralchicum 'Wisley'	200	600	yellow		April	✓		glossy green foliage	Stoloniferous dry shade
Epimedium versicolor 'Sulphureum'	400	600	yellow		April	✓			Stoloniferous dry shade
Euphorbia griffithii 'Dixter'	600	600	chestnut-tan		June		✓		
Fragaria vesca 'Variegata'	150	500	white		May		✓	striking variegated	Stoloniferous good ground cover between shrubs Alpine strawberries edible.
Geranium himalayense 'Gravetye'	300	300	blue				✓		
Geranium macrorrhizum album	500	500	off white		May	✓		scented leaf	

Name			Colour	Month	✓	Notes	✓	Comments
Geranium maculatum 'Chatto'	400	400	pink				✓	Early
Geranium 'Patrica'	600	700	magenta pink/indigo eye	June/July			✓	More compact than *G.psilostemon*
Geranium phaeum 'Samobor'	800	700	purple	June		chocolate blotched	✓	
Geum 'Coppertone'	200	200	copper	April			✓	
Geum 'Leonard's Variety'	300	200	red	April			✓	
Geum 'Lionel Cox'	200	200	apricot	April			✓	
Hacquetia epipactis	300	300	yellow	March			✓	
Iris japonica 'Ledger's Variety'	600	600	blue/yellow/white	April	✓	sickle shaped leaves		
Lamium 'White Nancy'	150	150	white	June	✓	silvered leaves		
Maianthemum bifolium subsp. *kamtschaticums*	300	500	white	April			✓	Stoloniferous
Mukdenia rossii	400	300	white	April			✓	
Pachyphragma macrophyllum	200	200	white	March			✓	
Persicaria affinis	150	200	pink	June	✓			Good ground cover between shrubs
Persicaria tenuicaulis	150	500	white	April			✓	
Phlox divaricata subsp. *Laphamii* 'Chattahoochee'	150	200	lilac	May	✓		✓	
Polygonatum odoratum var. *pluriflorum* 'Variegatum'	700	600	cream with green tips to leaves	April	✓	cream edge	✓	Pink shoots and stems
Polygonatum verticillatum rubrum	600	600	red	May	✓		✓	Red berries
Pulmonaria 'Blue Ensign'	300	300	Gentian blue	March		dark green foliage	✓	
Pulmonaria 'Diana Clare'	300	300	violet blue	March		long silver leaves	✓	

PLANT NAME	Height mm	Spread mm	Flower colour	Scent	Month of Flowering	Evergreen	Deciduous	Leaf Interest	COMMENTS
Pulmonaria officinalis 'Sissinghurst White'	300	300	white		March		✓	white spotted	
Ranunculus aconitifolius	600	600	white		May		✓		
Rheum 'Ace of Hearts'	1000	1000	cream		June		✓		
Saxifraga stolonifera 'Kinki Purple'	300	250	white		Aug/Sept		✓		
Speirantha convallarioides	200	300	white	✓	May		✓		
Symphytum ibericum	300	600	white		April	✓			Burnt orange flower buds Stoloniferous
Tellima grandiflora odorata	600	250	lime green	✓	June		✓		
Thalictrum delavayi album	700	300	white		July/August		✓		
Tiarella 'Pink Bouquet'	300	250	pink		April/May		✓		
Uvularia grandiflora var. *pallida*	400	300	lemon yellow		April		✓		
Viola 'Governor Herrick'	200	200	large blue		April/May		✓		
Viola labradorica	150	200	light purple		April		✓		Good ground cover between shrubs
Viola 'Peppered Palms'	150	200	blue flecked		April		✓	trifoliate	

FURTHER INFORMATION

LANDSCAPING SUPPLIERS

DMS Landscaping Supplies Topsoils, ornamental bark, aggregate, stone.
www.dmslandscapingsupplies.co.uk

Frimstone Ltd Aggregate extraction and supply of materials, including sand, gravel, topsoil, slate.
www.frimstone.co.uk

Gardenscape Direct Ltd Hard and soft landscape supplies.
www.gardenscapedirect.co.uk

Landscaping Supplies Ltd Aggregate, railway sleepers.
www.landscaping-supplies.net

Railway Sleeper.com Supplier of new and used hardwood and softwood railway sleepers.
www.railwaysleeper.com

Rowebb Garden Landscape Centres Garden aggregate, sleepers.
www.rowebb.com

UK Sleepers A wide range of traditional and reclaimed railway sleepers.
www.uksleepers.co.uk

Woodgrow Horticulture Topsoil, bark, aggregate.
www.woodgrow.com

PLANTS

Harveys Garden Plants The author's own family-run nursery, specializing in Hellebores, Heleniums and other perennials, particularly plants not commonly found garden centres.
www.harveysgardenplants.co.uk

Notcutts Huge nursery producing wide range of plants with garden centres in many parts of the UK.
www.notcutts.co.uk

Waterers Another large nursery producing a big selection of quality hardy plants available through a wide range of UK stockists.
www.waterersnursery.co.uk

David Austin Roses Major grower of quality roses, in particular breeder of many of the modern New English Roses.
www.davidaustinroses.com

INDEX

OTHER GARDENING BOOKS FROM CROWOOD